IN THE NAME OF

ALLAH

THE ALL-COMPASSIONATE, ALL-MERCIFUL

How to Make It
in Today's World

- Title: How to Make It in Today's World
- Author: Michael Tofte
- English Edition 2 (2014)
- Layout Design: IIPH, Riyadh, Saudi Arabia
- Cover Design: Samo Press Group, Beirut

HOW TO MAKE IT IN TODAY'S WORLD

A MODERN MUSLIM'S SURVIVAL GUIDE

النجاة في عالم اليوم
دليل للمسلم المعاصر

Michael Tofte

الدار العالمية للكتاب الإسلامي

INTERNATIONAL ISLAMIC PUBLISHING HOUSE

Copyright © 2014 International Islamic Publishing House
King Fahd National Library Cataloging-in-Publication Data

Tofte, Michael
    How to make it in today's world. / Michael Tofte. -2. - Riyadh,
2014

        240 pp ; 21 cm

        1- Islam and modernism   2- Modernism - religious
aspects - Islam   I- Title

        210.8 dc

Legal Deposit no. **1435/2375**
ISBN Hard cover: 978-603-501-241-6

International Islamic Publishing House (IIPH)
P.O. Box 55195 Riyadh 11534, Saudi Arabia
Tel: 966 1 4650818 / 4647213 — Fax: 966 1 4633489
E-mail: editorial@iiph.com — iiphsa@gmail.com
www.iiph.com | www.iiph.com.sa

TABLE OF CONTENTS

ARABIC HONORIFIC SYMBOLS USED IN THIS BOOK

(ﷻ): *Subḥânahu wa ta'âlâ* — 'The Exalted'

(ﷺ): *Ṣalla-Allâhu 'alayhi wa sallam* — 'Blessings and peace be upon him'

(ﷺ): *'Alayhis-salâm* — 'Peace be upon him'

(ؓ): *Raḍiya Allâhu 'anhu* — 'May Allah be pleased with <u>him</u>'

(ؓ): *Raḍiya Allâhu 'anhâ* — 'May Allah be pleased with <u>her</u>'

PRONUNCIATION AND TRANSLITERATION CHART

Arabic script	Pronunciation	Transliterated as:
أ	short 'a', as in *cat*	a
ى – آ	longer 'a', as in *cab* (not as in *cake*)	â
ب	/b/ as in *bell, rubber* and *tab*	b
ت	/t/ as in *tap, mustard* and *sit*	t
ة	takes the sound of the preceding diactrical mark sometimes ending in h (when in pausal form): ah, ih, or ooh; or atu(n), ati(n) or ata(n) when in uninterrupted speech	h or t (when followed by another Arabic word)
ث	/th/ as in *thing, maths* and *wealth*	th
ج	/j/ as in *jam, ajar* and *age*	j
ح	a 'harsher' sound than the English initial /h/, and may occur medially and in word-final position as well	ḥ
خ	as in *Bach* (in German); may occur initially and medially as well	kh
د	/d/ as in *do, muddy* and *red*	d
ذ	as in *this, father,* and *with*	dh
ر	/r/ as in *raw, art* and *war*; may also be a rolled r, as with Spanish words	r

Arabic script	Pronunciation	Transliterated as:
ز	/z/ as in *zoo*, *easy* and *gaze*	z
س	/s/ as in *so*, *messy* and *grass*	s
ش	as in *ship*, *ashes* and *rush*	sh
ص	no close equivalent in English, but may be approximated by pronouncing it as /sw/ or /s/ farther back in the mouth	ṣ
ض	no close equivalent in English, but may be approximated by pronouncing /d/ farther back in the mouth	ḍ
ط	no close equivalent in English, but may be approximated by pronouncing /t/ farther back in the mouth	ṭ
ظ	no close equivalent in English, but may be approximated by pronouncing 'the' farther back in the mouth	<u>dh</u>
ع	no close equivalent in English: a guttural sound in the back of the throat	ʿ
غ	no close equivalent in English, but may be closely approximated by pronouncing it like the French /r/ in 'rouge'	gh
ف	/f/ as in *fill*, *effort* and *muff*	f

Arabic script	Pronunciation	Transliterated as:
ق	no close equivalent in English, but may be approximated by pronouncing /k/ farther back in the mouth	q
ك	/k/ as in *king, buckle* and *tack*	k
ل	/l/ as in *lap, halo*; in the word *Allah*, it becomes velarized as in *ball*	l
م	/m/ as in *men, simple* and *ram*	m
ن	/n/ as in *net, ant* and *can*	n
ـﻪ – ﻩ – ﻬ	/h/ as in *hat*; unlike /h/ in English, in Arabic /h/ is pronounced in medial and word-final positions as well	h
و	as in *wet* and *away*	w
و (as a vowel)	long u, as in *boot* and *too*	oo
ي	as in *yet* and *yard*	y
ي (as a vowel)	long e, as in *eat, beef* and *see*	ee
ء	glottal stop: may be closely approximated by pronouncing it like 't' in the Cockney English pronunciation of *butter*: *bu'er*, or the stop sound in *uh — oh!*	' (Omitted in initial position)

Diphthongs:

Arabic script	Pronunciation	Transliterated as:
أَوَ ، و	Long o, as in *owe*, *boat* and *go*	au, aw, ow
أَي ، يَ	Long 'a', as in *able*, *rain* and *say*	ay, ai, ei

Diacritical marks (*tashkeel*):

Name of mark	Pronunciation	Transliterated as:
ـَ fathah	very short 'a' or schwa (unstressed vowel)	a
ـِ kasrah	shorter version of ee or schwa (unstressed vowel)	i
ـُ Dammah	shorter version of oo	u
ـّ shaddah	a doubled consonant is stressed in the word, and the length of the sound is also doubled	Double letter
ـْ sukoon	no vowel sound between consonants or at the end of a word	Absence of vowel

ABOUT THE WORD 'LORD'

$\mathcal{T}$he word *lord* in English has several related meanings. The original meaning is 'master' or 'ruler', and in this sense it is often used to refer to human beings: 'the lord of the mansion' or 'Lord So-and-So' (in the United Kingdom, for example). The word *Lord* with a capital L is used in the lexicon of Islam to refer to the One and Only God — Allah. In Islam, there is no ambiguity about the meaning of this word. While it is true that one may occasionally use the word *lord* (whether capitalized or not) to refer to a human being, in Islamic discourse the reference of this term is always clear from the context. Whereas for Christians, Hindus and other polytheists, the word *Lord* with a capital 'L' may refer to Allah, to Jesus or to some imagined deity, for Muslims, there can be no plurality of meaning. Allah alone is the Lord, and the Lord is Allah — not Jesus, not Rama, not any other being.

The Editor

The Islamic viewpoint
on slavery

$\mathscr{S}$ lavery existed before the coming of Prophet Muhammad (ﷺ). Islam did not abolish slavery, though it put limits on it and made it a virtuous act to free slaves.

In Islam, there is only one way a person may become enslaved and that is by being a non-Muslim among people who have been captured after raising arms and fighting against the Muslim nation. When such people have been conquered, the Muslim ruler has the option of enslaving them or releasing them (with or without ransom), and he makes this decision based upon the best interests and safety of the state. The Prophet (ﷺ) strongly rebuked any other means of enslaving a person. Thus, no person may become enslaved due to poverty, debt, kidnapping, committing a crime, voluntarily submitting to slavery, or any other means.

Islam encourages the freeing of slaves and has made the freeing of a slave a form of expiation for sins such as accidental manslaughter, the breaking of a vow, or voiding a fast by engaging in sexual intercourse. The freeing of slaves is also one of the categories upon which the zakâh funds should be spent (*Qur'an 9: 60*). The Qur'an calls the freeing of a slave an act of righteousness that may be performed at any time:

❨Righteous are those who believe in Allah, the Last Day, the angels, the scripture, and the prophets; and they give money, cheerfully, to the relatives, the orphans, the needy, the wayfarer, the beggars, and to free the slaves.》

(Qur'an 2: 177)

In regards to the treatment of slaves, the Prophet Muhammad (ﷺ) said: «They are your brothers whom Allah has put under your authority, so if Allah has put a person's brother under his authority, let him feed him from what he eats and clothe him from what he wears, and let him not overburden him with work, and if he does overburden him with work, then let him help him.» (Bukhari)

«Whoever accuses his slave when he is innocent of what he says will be flogged on the Day of Resurrection.» (Bukhari)

«Whoever slaps his slave or beats him, his expiation is to manumit him.» (Muslim)

«If a man had a slave woman whom he fed — and fed her well, and taught her — and taught her well, then he set her free and married her — he will have a double reward.» (Bukhari and Muslim)

The male owner of a female slave has the right to have sexual intercourse with her as long as he, or the slave's previous owner, has not married her to another person. This is a right exclusive to the slave's owner. No one, including the owner's sons, may touch the woman unless the owner marries her to him. If the slave woman bears her owner a child, then her owner may never sell her and she automatically becomes a free woman upon his death, if he has not released her before that.

As can be seen from this evidence, slavery in Islam is far different from the institution of slavery as known in many non-Muslim countries.

When jihad refers to fighting

Although jihad is often translated into English as 'holy war', it must be noted that war has never been described as 'holy' in any of Islam's primary texts or even early Islamic literature. Linguistically speaking, jihad is an Islamic term that applies to a broad spectrum of activities, ranging from daily striving to meet the day's challenges, to the striving against one's desires and self, to the struggle to provide for one's family. Its basic definition is 'the act of striving or struggling in the way of Allah'. Therefore, jihad is not limited to war; it includes struggling with one's soul, speech, body and wealth so that the message of Allah reaches all humans willing to receive it.

Islamic scholars have referred to different types of jihad, such as jihad against the self (to understand Islam, act upon it, call others to it and be patient with the difficulties of making this call), jihad against the Devil (repelling Satanic whispers, doubts and lusts), jihad against the tongue (controlling it, using it to enjoin what is good, forbid what is wrong, spread the correct teachings of Islam and answer false ideologies), jihad against aggression (with the purpose of protecting Islam and the lives, honour and property of Muslims) and other types of jihad like jihad against the hypocrites, jihad against oppressors and jihad against mischief makers.

Jihad — in the context of fighting — has specific rules and conditions that need to be met before jihad is initiated. The first rule is that people are not to be fought because of what they believe, or to coerce them to accept Islam. The second rule is to 'fight only those who fight you' and never initiate unprovoked aggression *(Qur'an 2: 190)*. That means that Muslims are only allowed to fight back, rather than initiating fighting; but 'fighting back' includes fighting against actual aggression as well as proactively addressing real threats of aggression. In both cases, Muslims are instructed to be prepared and ready to defend their nation before they actually engage in military conflict. There are other conditions that this book will discuss, but the above-mentioned conditions are vital for putting jihad in its broader meaning in the proper context.

Another condition of the sort of jihad which involves fighting is that it should take place only under an Islamic authority that 'raises the banner' for such jihad. It is not following the Sunnah at all for any individual or self-appointed group of Muslims to wage war on behalf of a nation. Instead, Muslims should be united under the single authority of an imam or khaleefah (caliph), except in the case where an individual needs to defend his own family and property, or to help his neighbour to do so. This is proved by the example of the early Muslims as well as texts in the Qur'an and the Sunnah:

⁅When there comes to them [the hypocrites] a matter related to [public] safety or fear, they spread it about; if only they had referred it to the Messenger and to such of them as are in authority, those among them who are able to think through the matter would have understood it.⁆

(Qur'an 4: 83)

«Hudhayfah ibn Yaman asked the Prophet (ﷺ): What if (the Muslims) have no single leader (they are divided into disputing groups)? The Prophet (ﷺ) answered: If they have no single leader or unified group, then leave all these disputing groups, even if you have to bite on a tree until your death.» (part of a longer hadith recorded by Bukhari)

There are other conditions for jihad. In general, the rules laid out for war in Islam should be upheld unless there is some legitimate need or strategy when fighting occurs that would necessitate going against those rules. A Muslim should not kill himself or herself *(Qur'an 4: 29)* nor kill another Muslim, except by accident *(Qur'an 4: 92)*. Women, children, the elderly and other non-combatants should not be harmed. Land should not be destroyed, nor trees cut down. Corpses should not be mutilated. Islam should not be imposed upon non-believers. Rather, if combatant non-Muslims choose on their own to embrace Islam, even if only as a deceitful trick, it should be accepted by the Muslim leadership, and fighting should stop. Peace should be sought before lives are lost. Treaties and agreements should be upheld. Prisoners should be well-treated. Above all, justice must be done.

❲Fight in the path [according to the rules set by Allah] of Allah only those who fight you, but do not commit aggression [transgress limits]. Allah does not love aggressors....And fight them until persecution is no more, and religion is [freely embraced] for [the individual's faith in] Allah. But if they desist, then let there be no aggression except against transgressors.❳   *(Qur'an 2: 190, 193)*

❲Allah does not forbid you from being good, kind, just, and fair to those who have not fought you because of religion nor driven you from your homeland. Allah loves those who are just. Allah forbids you from giving allegiance to those who have fought you because of religion and have driven you from your homeland, and those who supported your expulsion...❳   *(Qur'an 60: 8-9)*

In addition, the Muslim nation is encouraged to maintain strong military capabilities to promote justice and to deter acts of war and aggression.

❲And make ready for them [their potential aggression] all you can of power, including steeds of war, to deter the enemy of Allah and your enemy, and others besides, whom you may not know but whom Allah knows.❳   *(Qur'an 8: 60)*

PUBLISHER'S NOTE

*A*ll praise and thanks belongs to Allah alone, the One, the Almighty and All-Merciful. Blessings and peace be upon Prophet Muhammad, the last of His Messengers and Prophets, and upon his family, his Companions and all those who follow in his footsteps until the end of time.

Muslims today, especially those living in the West, face a variety of pressing issues. We recognize that the prophets and the believers throughout time have experienced hardships, and that the solution is to strive to live according to the Book of Allah and the example of our Prophet. However, it is not always easy to determine precisely how to apply Islamic teachings in a specific situation.

In this book, Brother Michael Tofte has addressed some of the common problems encountered by contemporary Muslims. Drawing on his study of Islamic sciences and his work within his American Muslim community, the author identifies the probable reasons for these troubles and then offers practical, realistic solutions.

We hope that the reader will benefit by being able to prevent such difficulties as much as possible. When a problem does arise, we hope that the information provided here will allow him or her to arrive at a resolution before it can turn into a full-blown crisis.

May Allah accept the efforts of all those who contributed to the production of this book, and may it be acceptable to Him, *âmeen*.

Muhammad ibn 'Abdul Mohsin Al-Tuwaijri

Managing Director
International Islamic Publishing House
Riyadh, Saudi Arabia

PREFACE

$\mathcal{T}$he praise is due solely to Allah (*Subhânahu wa Ta'âlâ* — Glorified and Exalted is He).[1] We seek His[2] help and His forgiveness. We seek refuge with Allah (ﷻ) from the evil of our own souls and from our bad deeds. Whomsoever Allah (ﷻ) guides will never be led astray, and whomsoever Allah (ﷻ) leaves to go astray, no one can guide. I bear witness that there is no god but Allah, the One, having no partner, and I bear witness that Muhammad (*Ṣalla Allâhu 'alayhi wa sallam* — blessings and peace be upon him)[3] is His slave and Messenger.

---

[1] The term 'Allah' does not refer exclusively to a Muslim God. 'Allah' is merely the Arabic term for the Supreme Being and Creator, whom English-speakers call God. Traditionally, Muslims, Jews, and Christians in the Arabic-speaking world all called God 'Allah'. In fact, Jesus (*'alayhi as-salâm* — peace be upon him) never used the word God; he would have used the Aramaic term 'Alaha'. For example, if the name God was not translated in the Bible, then the verse Matthew 4:10 would read, "The Lord **Alaha** is one God, and Him alone you shall serve/worship" instead of "The Lord our God is one God, and Him alone shall you serve/worship." This is a historical fact that can be verified by asking any Biblical scholar, or simply by looking at an Aramaic-language Bible with English translation and transliteration (which can be found on the Internet).

[2] We use the masculine pronoun 'His' because that is what the Arabic texts use. In Arabic and most other languages, masculine pronouns include the feminine, but feminine pronouns do not include the masculine. Of course, Allah has no gender; He is neither male nor female. He is is the Creator of both male and female and is high above having gender.

[3] Whenever a Muslim says the name of the Prophet Muhammad, he or she=

The most truthful speech is the book of Allah, and the best of guidance is that of Muhammad (ﷺ). The worst of evils are the newly invented matters in the religion. Every innovated matter is an innovation, every innovation is a misguidance, and every misguidance is in the hellfire.

In the name of Allah, the Most Gracious, the Most Merciful. All praises are due to Allah, the Lord of the universe and all that exists within it as well as outside of it. I seek only His assistance, and I seek only His guidance, in taking on the endeavour of writing this book. As all of the prophets, including Jesus (*'alayhi as-salâm —* peace be upon him)[4] and Muhammad (ﷺ), taught, I cannot do anything without His help. I cannot move, type, write, or even think without His help. Nothing happens except what He has decreed. Without Him, I could not even think of writing this book, so I praise Him for this tremendous opportunity to bring benefit to myself and to the Muslim community as well. I pray that this book serves as a source of guidance and benefit to the people of the world — both Muslims and non-Muslims. I ask Allah to accept this deed from me and to purify my intention while I write it, and I ask Him to keep this deed in accordance with the *Sunnah* (practice and collected sayings) of the Prophet Muhammad (ﷺ). Next, I pray that Allah showers his blessings on His last and final messenger Muhammad (ﷺ), as well as his family and his Companions (may Allah be pleased with them).[5]

I undertook the journey of writing this book for two reasons. First, I am inspired by the *hadith* (recorded saying or action of

---

=should pray for him by asking God to bless him, have mercy on him, and grant him peace.

[4] A prayer that Muslims say after the name of any other Prophet

[5] When we mention the names of the companions of the Prophet (and sometimes members of the following two generations and other pious people), we say, "May Allah be pleased with them."

Prophet Muhammad) in which Abu Hurayrah (ﷺ) reported that the Prophet (ﷺ) said: «When a person dies, all his good deeds cease except for three: a continuous act of charity, beneficial knowledge, and a righteous son (child) who prays for him.» (Muslim) I hope to leave behind beneficial knowledge that will bring me rewards even after I am dead.

Secondly, there is a lack of resources on this topic in the English language, despite the fact that it is one of the most important topics in all of Islam. My goal is to write a book that is simple, yet comprehensive, and that is in complete accordance with the Sunnah of Prophet Muhammad (ﷺ), so that all Muslims (but especially those in the West) can benefit from it.

Michael Tofte

INTRODUCTION

$\mathcal{T}$he Muslims of our Ummah today, especially those living in the West and in non-Muslim communities elsewhere, are faced with a variety of serious problems and challenges. We need to examine some of the causes of these problems that affect our society, and we need to seek out Islamic methods that can be used to solve them. The information in this book relates to all Muslims, whether young or old, immigrant or indigenous, convert, revert, or those who were born into a Muslim family. It even transcends religion, because many of the issues dealt with in this book are simply human issues.

Each topic here is dealt with briefly and concisely. In other words, I cut out the appetizers, the salad, the dessert, and the tea and go right to the steak (the 'meat' of the matter). When books are too long, people may simply put them on their shelves and receive no benefit from them; I feel that all of this information is needed by the Muslims, so I covered these issues in one short volume. I hope that this material will clear up several common misconceptions, without being apologetic.

We will delve into the important rights of parents, children, spouses, neighbours, other Muslims, and all human beings, according to the Qur'an and Sunnah. For example, when talking about parents and children, we will deal with such issues as: what causes children to be rebellious, when it is the parent's fault, what children can do if their rights are not granted, and when children can legitimately disobey their parents.

Respecting the rights of others is very important when it comes to preventing and solving problems. Many of our problems in life come from our interactions with other people, and most of our problems with people stem from not following the Sunnah. Short, easy to read chapters will suggest preventive measures, because often the best way to solve one's problems is to learn what is causing them and to cut them off at the root before they blossom into a field of troubles.

In one chapter, we walk through a day in the life of the Prophet (ﷺ), from the time he woke up in the morning all the way until his late night prayers. It is necessary to know how he lived, because if we followed his example, many — if not most — of our problems would disappear, and we would be more happy, content, and successful in this life and the next.

We recognize that many of our problems, and their solutions, have their roots in both the physical and spiritual worlds. The next chapter analyzes the spiritual causes of our problems and gives practical methods to be applied in the physical world to protect ourselves from the spiritual war in which we are engaged with our satanic enemies; it also teaches us how to acquire spiritual help from the angelic realm.

Next are chapters dealing with communal issues that we face, for which Muslims need clear explanations and solutions. I will describe the proper methods for correcting the actions of others, according to the Sunnah. This topic is especially important today since many Muslims are trying to correct people's actions without proper knowledge and understanding, and this leads to a plethora of problems within Muslim communities.

After that, I consider the issues of backbiting, spying, and not verifying information before spreading it (an issue which is plaguing local and global communities). I will define these terms, since many do not know exactly what terms such as 'backbiting' mean. This chapter leads perfectly into our next chapter, which explains how to purify the seven limbs (the eyes, ears, tongue, stomach, private parts, hands and feet) and provides exercises that can help us to remove most sins from our lives.

Next, we tackle the pressing political and social issues of the modern world, by showing what the Prophet (ﷺ) had to say about them. This chapter will deal with issues such as Palestine, Iraq, Chechnya, terrorism, globalization, pop culture, the sexual revolution, the boom in technology and industrialization. The Prophet (ﷺ) told us about all of these things that were going to occur and explained why they would occur. His Sunnah left us guidance in all of these areas of life.

Since we all need help with life's decisions, the Prophet (ﷺ) provided us with a prayer asking Allah to guide us in all of our decisions. A chapter is devoted to this prayer.

The next chapter discusses many of the good deeds with which we can occupy our time, in order to avoid the major problems that exist in our life.

The Arabic word *eemân*, which is generally translated as faith, also means safety and security. The more your faith in Allah (ﷺ) increases, the more safe and secure you feel inside. The Qur'an and hadiths teach us that following the Sunnah completely is the way to have complete eemân. Eemân is the key to handling problems when they arise. Therefore, the formula is simple: the more of the Sunnah you implement and practice in your life, the more your eemân increases; the more your eemân increases, the more you can handle and overcome problems that arise.

This whole book is based on the Sunnah. It teaches us how to apply the Sunnah in our personal lives, our social lives and our political lives. The Sunnah is the key to a happy life and the key to a happy afterlife. If we follow the Sunnah, we will have inner peace and prosperity. If we abandon the Sunnah, we will have problem after problem in our lives.

After finishing this book, it is hoped that both Muslim and non-Muslim readers will understand where all of the problems in their personal life — as well as in the world — stem from and will know how to solve them.

Methods of Solving Problems

$\mathcal{T}$o deal with the problems we face, the Prophet (ﷺ) gave us advice regarding physical, spiritual and social aspects of life. In addition, the Prophet's Companions (may Allah be pleased with them) and the earlier scholars shared with us their contemplations, in which we can find other problem-solving techniques based on the Qur'an and Sunnah. There are at least five components to handling the challenges and difficulties we face.

1. The first component of problem-solving is following specific physical advice from the Prophet (ﷺ)

He (ﷺ) gave us advice in dealing with anger from a physical perspective: «It is reported that the Messenger of Allah (ﷺ) said that while Sulayman was with the Prophet (ﷺ), two persons were blaming each other. The face of one became red, and his jugular veins swelled. The Prophet (ﷺ) said: I know a statement that, if he or she says it, then the person with anger will cool down. The person with anger should say: *A'oodhu billâhi minash-shayṭânir-rajeem* (I seek refuge in Allah from Satan the outcast).» (Bukhari and Muslim)

Abu Dharr al-Ghifâri narrated that the Messenger of Allah (ﷺ) said: «When one of you is angry, if he is standing then let him sit down, and if his anger abates (then well and good), otherwise let him lie down.» (a sound hadith recorded by Abu Dâwood)

The Prophet (ﷺ) said: «Anger is from the devil, the devil was created from fire, and only water extinguishes fire. Therefore, if one of you becomes angry, let him perform ablution.» (a reliable hadith recorded by Aḥmad and Abu Dâwood)

2. The second component to removing a problem is to repent

Ask Allah (ﷻ) for forgiveness for the action and continuously make supplications for the cause of the problem (the spiritual disease causing the problem) to be removed. Supplications, or prayers where one asks Allah for something, can be done at any time by anyone, in any language.

The Prophet Muhammad's statements regarding repentance

Al-Agharr ibn Yassâr al-Muzani (﵁) narrated that the Messenger of Allah (ﷺ) said: «Turn, you people, in repentance to Allah (ﷻ), and beg pardon of Him. I turn to Him in repentance a hundred times a day.» (Muslim)

Abu Moosâ al-Ash'ari (﵁) reported that the Prophet (ﷺ) said: «Allah will continue to stretch out His Hand in the night so that the sinners of the day may repent, and continue to stretch His Hand in the daytime so that the sinners of the night may repent, until the sun rises from the west.» (Muslim)

Anas (﵁) narrated that Allah's Messenger (ﷺ) said: «Allah (ﷻ) has said: O son of Adam, I shall go on forgiving you as long as you pray to Me and aspire for My forgiveness, whatever may be your faults. O son of Adam, I do not care even if your sins should pile up to the sky; should you beg pardon of Me, I would forgive you. O son of Adam, if you come to me with an earthful of sins and meet Me, not associating anything with Me (in worship), I will come to you with an earthful of forgiveness.» (a sound hadith recorded by at-Tirmidhi)

Abu Sa'eed al-Khudri (﵁) reported that the Prophet of Allah (ﷺ) said: «There was a person before you who had killed ninety-nine persons and then made an inquiry about the learned persons of the world (who could show him the way to salvation). He was directed to a monk. He went to him and told him that he had killed ninety-nine persons, and asked him whether there was any scope for his repentance to be accepted. The monk said no. The man killed the monk also, and thus completed one hundred. He then asked about the learned persons of the earth, and he was directed to a scholar. He told the scholar that he had killed one hundred persons and asked him whether there was any scope for his repentance to be accepted. The scholar said: Yes — what stands between you and the repentance? You had better go to such and such land; there are people devoted to prayer and worship. You also worship along with them, and do not return to your land, since it was an evil land (for you). So the man went away, and he had hardly covered half the distance when death came to him. There was a dispute between the angels of mercy and the angels of punishment. The angels of mercy said: This man has come as a penitent and remorseful to Allah (ﷻ), and the angels of punishment said: He has done no good at all. Then there came another angel in the form of a human being, in order to decide between them. He said: Measure the land to which he has drawn near. They measured it and found him nearer to the land where he intended to go (the land of piety), and so the angels of mercy took possession of him.» (Bukhari and Muslim)

Conditions for repentance

There are conditions for one's repentance to be accepted:
1) Quitting the sinful behaviour immediately
2) Feeling truly and sincerely sorry and regretful for having committed the sin
3) Promising oneself and truly intending never to do it again
4) If it relates to the rights of another person, restoring their rights or property and/or seeking their forgiveness

For condition number four, in cases where you talked about someone behind their back, and the person does not even know it, scholars have different opinions about whether you should ask him or her for forgiveness. If telling the person will cause greater harm or greater damage to your relationship, then ask for forgiveness only from Allah (ﷻ). However, if the person is not the type to hold a grudge, then ask him or her for forgiveness as well.

It is highly recommended to do good deeds to make up for the bad deeds that one has done. Abu Dharr (Jundub ibn Junâdah) and Abu 'Abdur-Raḥmân (Mu'âdh ibn Jabal) (may Allah be pleased with them) reported that the Messenger of Allah (ﷺ) said: «Fear Allah wherever you may be; follow up an evil deed with a good one, which will wipe it (the former) out; and behave good-naturedly towards people.» (a reliable hadith recorded by at-Tirmidhi)

The Qur'an tells us:

❴Indeed, the men who practice charity and the women who practice charity and [they who] have loaned Allah a goodly loan — it will be multiplied for them, and they will have a noble reward.❵

(Qur'an 57: 18) [6]

❴Whoever comes [on the Day of Judgment] with a good deed will have ten times the like thereof [to his credit], and whoever comes with an evil deed will not be recompensed except the like thereof, and they will not be wronged.❵   *(Qur'an 6: 160)*

When are the best times to make supplications?

The last third of the night

Abu Hurayrah (ﷺ) narrated that Allah's Messenger (ﷺ) said: «In the last third of every night, our Lord descends to the lowermost

---

[6] The translations of the meanings of the verses of the Qur'an in this book are taken (with some changes to the text) from: Ṣaḥeeḥ International, *The Quran: Arabic Text with Corresponding English Meanings*, Riyadh: Abul Qasim Publishing House, 1997.

heaven and says: Who is calling Me, so that I may answer him? Who is asking Me, so that may I grant him? Who is seeking forgiveness from Me, so that I may forgive him?» (Bukhari)

'Amr ibn Absah (ﷺ) narrated that the Prophet (ﷺ) said: «The closest any worshipper can be to His Lord is during the last part of the night, so if you can be amongst those who remember Allah (ﷺ) at that time, then do so.» (a sound hadith recorded by at-Tirmidhi, an-Nasâ'i and al-Ḥâkim)

Between the first and second calls to prayer

Anas (ﷺ) narrated that Allah's Messenger (ﷺ) said: «A supplication made between the first call to prayer and the second call to prayer is not rejected.» (a sound hadith recorded by Aḥmad, Abu Dâwood, at-Tirmidhi, an-Nasâ'i and Ibn Ḥibbân)

While prostrating

Abu Hurayrah (ﷺ) narrated that Allah's Messenger (ﷺ) said: «The nearest a slave can be to his Lord is when he is prostrating, so invoke Allah much in it.» (Muslim, Abu Dâwood, an-Nasâ'i)

After the obligatory prayers

«Abu Umamah (ﷺ) narrated that Allah's Messenger (ﷺ) was asked: O Messenger of Allah, which supplication is heard? He said: the end of the night and at the end of the obligatory prayer.» (a reliable hadith recorded by at-Tirmidhi)

When it is raining

Sahl ibn Sa'ad (ﷺ) narrated that the Messenger of Allah (ﷺ) said: «Two supplications will not be rejected: when the first call to prayer is being called, and at the time of rain.» (a reliable hadith recorded by al-Hâkim, Abu Dâwood, and Ibn Mâjah)

«Seek the response to your supplications when the armies meet, when the prayer is called, and when rain falls.» (a reliable hadith recorded by Imam Shâfi'i in *al-Umm*)

When fasting or being oppressed

The Prophet (ﷺ) declared: «Three whose supplication is never rejected [by Allah (ﷻ)] are: the fasting person until he or she breaks the fast (in another narration: when he or she breaks the fast), the just ruler, and the one who is oppressed.» (a sound hadith recorded by Ahmad and at-Tirmidhi)

The Messenger of Allah (ﷺ) said to Mu'âdh ibn Jabal (رضي الله عنه): «Beware of the supplication of the unjustly treated, because there is no shelter or veil between it (the supplication of the one who is suffering injustice) and Allah (ﷻ).» (Bukhari and Muslim)

The parent and the traveler

The Messenger of Allah (ﷺ) said: «Three supplications will not be rejected: the supplication of the parent for his child, the supplication of the one who is fasting, and the supplication of the traveler.» (a reliable hadith recorded by Bayhaqi and at-Tirmidhi)

Start with praising Allah and praying for the Prophet (ﷺ)

«When any one of you makes supplications, let him start by glorifying his Lord and praising Him. Then let him send blessings upon the Prophet (ﷺ); then let him pray for whatever he wants.» (a sound hadith recorded by Abu Dâwood and at-Tirmidhi)

«Ibn Mas'ood (رضي الله عنه) narrated: I was once praying, and the Prophet (ﷺ), Abu Bakr and 'Umar (رضي الله عنهما) (were all present). When I sat down (in the final testification of faith), I praised Allah, then sent *salâms* (greetings of peace) on the Prophet, then started praying for myself. At this, the Prophet (ﷺ) said: Ask, and you shall be given it! Ask, and you shall be given it!» (a sound hadith recorded by at-Tirmidhi)

Sincerely asking Allah (ﷻ) to give to someone else that which you desire

The Prophet (ﷺ) said: «There is no believing servant who supplicates for his brother in his absence where the angels do not say: the same be for you.» (Muslim)

3. The third component to solving one's problems is to keep good company

The third component to solving one's problems is to keep company with people who do not have the problem you have and who already have the attributes that you are trying to acquire. The more time you spend with them, the more you acquire their characteristics.

Abu Hurayrah (ﷺ) reported that he heard the Prophet (ﷺ) say: «Man follows his friend's religion; you should be careful whom you take for friends.» (a reliable hadith recorded by at-Tirmidhi and Abu Dâwood)

Abu Moosâ al-Ash'ari (ﷺ) reported that he heard the Prophet (ﷺ) say: «The similitude of good company and that of bad company is that of the owner of musk and of the one blowing the bellows (the blacksmith). The owner of musk either offers you some free of charge, or you buy it from him, or you smell its pleasant fragrance; as for the one who blows the bellows, he either burns your clothes or you smell a repugnant smell.» (Bukhari and Muslim)

Abu Sa'eed al-Khudri (ﷺ) reported that the Prophet (ﷺ) said: «Keep only a believer for a companion, and let only a pious person eat your food.» (a reliable hadith recorded by at-Tirmidhi and Abu Dâwood)

«Ibn Mas'ood (رضي الله عنه) reported: A man came to Messenger of Allah (ﷺ) and said: O Messenger of Allah! What do you think of a man who loves some people but does not get any nearer to their position (cannot attain their lofty position of righteousness)? He (ﷺ) replied: A person will be with those whom he loves.» (Bukhari and Muslim)

4. The fourth component of problem-solving comprises psychological strategies

The fourth component of problem-solving comprises psychological strategies for removing diseases of the heart, which are the spiritual and psychological causes behind many issues. These are pieces of advice from our predecessors (may Allah be pleased with them). We will not refer to hadiths; these are simply points for one to think deeply about. Any disease of the heart is in actuality a result of warped thinking, and it indicates a lack of understanding of *tawheed*.

Tawheed can be translated as monotheism, or the belief in one God. In English-speaking societies, when people are asked "Do you believe in God?", many will say yes. However, if they are asked, "What does that mean?" the only answer many people give is, "God created me, and He knows who I am."

Tawheed is much deeper than that. Yes, Allah (ﷻ) is the Creator of everything other than Himself, but Allah (ﷻ) is more than that. He had no beginning and will never end, while all of His creation has a beginning. Allah is independent and needs nothing to survive, while all of His creatures depend on something else for their survival. Allah (ﷻ) is perfect and never changes, while His creation is imperfect and constantly changing. Allah (ﷻ) is different from everything else.

Allah knows everything; He willed and decreed everything that has ever happened and will ever happen, and everything occurs for reasons that He knows. All other conscious beings have limitations to their knowledge; they do not know everything.

Allah (ﷻ) is the source of power behind every action; no one can move or even breathe independent of His power. He (ﷻ) gives us everything, including the power to think, move and act. Allah is constantly maintaining the universe, the worlds, the various dimensions and everything in them. Nothing acts independently of His will. We are born when Allah decreed for us to be born, and we die on the day that Allah decreed for us to die. Everything we have — material, physical or spiritual — is from Allah (ﷻ), and we will never get more than what Allah has decreed for us.

Nothing and no one can help us or harm us except Allah (ﷻ). No one is truly in control or truly has power except Allah (ﷻ). Everything in existence that does help us is only helping us by the will of Allah and by the power that He (ﷻ) gave to it.

Despite the claims of some contemporary speakers that tawheed can be taught in five minutes, there was a reason that the Prophet Muhammad (ﷺ) taught it for twenty-three years. It is no coincidence that most of the greatest of his Companions (may Allah be pleased with them) accepted Islam during the Makkan period. They had the purest hearts because the knowledge of tawheed was being poured into their hearts over and over again. They were the most saturated with the knowledge and understanding of tawheed. When one **truly** understands tawheed, most of these diseases will disappear. Our hearts are like dishes that have not been washed in years, and tawheed is like water and a cleansing agent. The more we

clean our hearts with tawḥeed, the cleaner they become. By
constantly drinking from the spring of tawḥeed, we can eventually
scrub all forms of *shirk* (associating partners with Allah),[7]
innovations in religion,[8] and cultural *jâhiliyah*[9] from our hearts.

5. The fifth component is daily recitation of the Qur'an

The Qur'an itself states:

❨We send down in the Qur'an that which is a healing and a mercy for
those who believe.❩   *(Qur'an 17: 82)*

❨...It is, for those who believe, a guidance and cure...❩ *(Qur'an 41: 44)*

Set aside some time every day to recite the Qur'an, whether it
is one minute or one hour. It can be at the same time every day or at
random times, whenever you get a break. One technique that has
been used by some modern Muslims is to recite the Qur'an one verse
at a time, once in Arabic and then again in their native tongue (if it is
not Arabic). This method has brought success to many people that I
know.

---

[7] For an explanation of shirk, see the section about it in the next chapter.

[8] Ideas or practices that some Muslims have made a part of their life, which
go against the teachings and practices of the Prophet (ﷺ) and his
Companions (may Allah be pleased with them).

[9] There are two types of jâhiliyah (ignorance): restricted and unrestricted.
Unrestricted jâhiliyah refers to the period of time before the angel Jibreel
(عليه السلام) brought down the revelation to the Prophet Muhammad (ﷺ). This is
when the world was void of the pure teachings of tawḥeed. This period is
over and will never return. However, there are restricted forms of jâhiliyah.
These are cultural practices of Muslims that violate the teachings of the
Islamic Sharia (law) and the Sunnah.

The Causes of All Our Problems

$\mathcal{T}$he problems faced by all people — Muslim and non-Muslim — have root causes. Through the Qur'an and Sunnah, Islam teaches us the root causes of all of our problems and then provides solutions for them. In the following sections, we will discuss the specific origins of many of our problems, and how the Prophet (ﷺ) and his inheritors taught us to solve each of them.

Anger

There are two types of anger in Islam: that which is praiseworthy and that which is blameworthy. They have different causes and often have different effects on the body.

When you see idolatry, injustice, and sin, you should get angry; however, the anger should not be tied to your ego. There is no rage involved; this anger is closer to what might be called disapproval in Western culture. If you have praiseworthy anger, and you advise the wrongdoer, you are naturally disappointed if the person does not listen. However, you do not scream, yell or physically attack the person (except in self-defense). You should merely walk away and pray that the person changes his or her ways.

On the other hand, those who are actually angry for the sake of their own ego — and not solely for the sake of Allah (ﷻ) — may engage in a screaming match or a physical fight, and they may take it personally when the person does not listen. Blameworthy anger drains one physically and emotionally after the anger subsides, which is not the case with praiseworthy anger. The techniques below are cures for blameworthy anger only, because praiseworthy anger does not need to be cured.

In the last chapter, I discussed the three techniques taught by the Prophet Muhammad (ﷺ): say a'oodhu billâhi minash-shaytânir-rajeem (I seek refuge in Allah from Satan the outcast); if you are standing, sit; and if you are sitting, lie down; and make ablution.

Many scholars of our religion were also medical doctors. Some recommended that after doing these things that the Prophet (ﷺ) recommended, you should drink cool water. This is merely medical advice; drinking cool water is not a substitute for the other actions, nor is it a part of our religion, and it is not to be done until after the other techniques. Nonetheless, when you get angry, the body temperature rises, and this can have harmful effects on your body. The water cools the body down physiologically and reduces the harmful effects of excess heat in your body.

Repent for any actions done in a state of anger, and make supplications to Allah (ﷻ) (especially at the best times for making supplications) to cure you of anger.

Spend time with people who are not easily angered, so that their characteristics have an effect on you.

Practice as many of the daily remembrances of Allah (ﷻ) and the practices of the Prophet Muhammad (ﷺ) as you are able.

Reflect[10] on death. Think about the fact that you could die at any second. If you were on your deathbed right now, would these things really be worth getting infuriated about? If you lived each moment as if it were your last, would you want to spend your last

---

[10] Throughout this book, I use the word 'reflect' many times. What this means is that you should think about it a great deal. Think about it while driving. Read certain verses or hadiths every day, maybe many times per day. Sit sometimes and just think about the meanings of those verses and hadiths, or about the advice given in this book. Say it out loud. Continue this until the disease is removed from your heart.

moment angry about this? If you were dying, the things that make you angry would most likely not even faze you, much less anger you.

Recite from the noble Qur'an daily.

Arrogance

Arrogance is a very serious sin that has plagued humankind for millennia, and the Prophet (ﷺ) gave us a stern warning about it. «He (ﷺ) stated: One will not enter paradise if one has an atom's weight of arrogance in his or her heart. A man then asked: One may love his clothes to look good and his shoes to look good? The Prophet replied: Allah is beautiful and loves beauty; arrogance is rejecting the truth and looking down on people.» (Muslim)

There are two types of arrogance. The first is when one refuses to accept the truth despite knowing that it is true; the second is looking down on others.

Many Christians are very guilty of the first type of arrogance. They pray to Jesus (ﷺ) and to various saints, they make images of Allah (both in paintings and statues), and some even go as far as to say that Jesus (ﷺ) is God. When someone, whether Christian or Muslim, brings them proof from their own Bible — and from common sense — pointing out that Jesus is not Allah (ﷺ), that one can only pray to Allah alone (and not to saints), that making a statue or painting representing Allah (ﷺ) is a worse evil than murder and adultery (according to their own scriptures), and that all of these actions (if done with knowledge that they are wrong) will cause someone to go to hell forever (even according to their own Christian Bible), they reject what their own Bible says and continue these practices anyway. They reject the advice out of arrogance, emotion and insincerity towards Allah. If Allah throws them in hell forever, they deserve it because they had knowledge of the truth, but they rejected it.

Many Muslims are also guilty of this type of arrogance. The Prophet (ﷺ) said: «If someone whose piety and character you are satisfied with comes to you, marry (an eligible female) to him. If you do not do so, there will be trials in the earth and a great deal of evil (or: you will spread trials and corruption throughout the earth).» (a reliable hadith recorded by at-Tirmidhi)

Many so-called Muslims (especially from certain parts of the Muslim world) refuse to marry their daughters to other Muslims with whom they pray and eat, simply because the men have different skin colors than them or come from different ethnic backgrounds, cultures, castes, tribes, or regions of the same country. If pious Muslim men come to them, they refuse to marry their daughters to them on these grounds, even after hearing the hadith mentioned above. Some do so because they have diseased hearts and they fear the people more than they fear Allah (ﷻ). In their hearts, they want to do the right thing, but they do not have the courage to stand up to the other family members who are enjoining the wrong and forbidding the right. Others are actually committing shirk, because in their hearts, they do not want to do the right thing. They believe that the customs and rules of their culture are over and above the rules of Allah; in this sense, they have made their customs or their culture a partner with Allah (ﷻ). If Allah (ﷻ) puts these individuals in hell forever, they deserve it because they know the truth and consciously choose to reject it.

To cure this first type of arrogance, you must repent from your wrongs and restate your Islamic testimony of faith. (This does not have to be done publicly; it can be done in private.) You need to make supplications to Allah (ﷻ) sincerely, asking for His divine help. You must look for sincere, righteous company to spend your time with. You should frequent the mosque more and practice as many recommended acts as you can every day.

Concerning the second type of arrogance, looking down on others, there are seven things that people are mainly arrogant about: lineage and race, strength and size, wealth, worldly power, beauty, education and religious works.

Signs of arrogance

❖ You do not want to spend time with, or be close to, people of different ethnic backgrounds, people who have less wealth or education than you, people who are less attractive than you, or people who have less worldly power or status than you.

❖ You do not like to walk alone; you prefer to have others follow you.

❖ You want your servants, spouse, or children to do everything for you.

❖ You cannot accept someone else's opinion, even when you know that it is correct.

❖ You refuse to marry your children to someone of a different ethnicity, race or culture.

❖ You have assumptions about certain groups of people of different races, ethnicities, or cultures when you meet them.

❖ You mock people of other ethnic groups or cultures.

❖ You do not greet Muslims of certain races, ethnic groups or social classes with the Islamic greeting *as-salâmu 'alaykum* (peace be upon you).

❖ You assume that people of certain ethnic groups are less educated, criminal, poor, and the like, just because of their skin color or the part of the world that they come from.

❖ You use skin lightening cream to change your complexion. (This shows that you feel inferior to lighter skinned people and arrogant towards darker skinned people.)

❖ Your body language and facial expressions towards certain people demonstrate your subconscious or conscious arrogance.

❖ You do not invite members of certain groups or social classes to events.

❖ You are not interested in hearing what others have to say.

❖ You are judgmental or see yourself as better than others because they have committed certain sins that you have not, or they have certain faults that you do not.

❖ You are 'self-satisfied' and do not seek to improve yourself.

❖ You are 'stuck in your ways'.

❖ You like for people to stand up to greet you.

How to know if you are arrogant

☞ Evaluate yourself. Look for the signs of arrogance and honestly state to yourself whether or not you have them.

☞ Find someone you know who is humble, and ask him or her to examine your conduct and your speech for signs of arrogance.

☞ Go to people who have a history of being the targets of arrogance, and ask them to search your conduct and speech for signs of arrogance. For example, in the United States, people have been arrogant towards African-Americans. As a result, many African-Americans have developed a keen sense of how to detect arrogance, racism, prejudice and the like. Because of cultural experiences, they may have more knowledge in this area than other native born Americans or members of most immigrant populations. You should not assume that just because someone is African-American, he or she possesses this knowledge, though; likewise, you should not assume that just because a person is white, Arab or South Asian, that he or she does not have this knowledge. This assumption itself is also a type of arrogance, which is found in many people from minority groups that have a history of being discriminated against.

Medicines for arrogance

If your arrogance is due to pride in your lineage, reflect on the story of Adam (ﷺ) and Satan, and how Satan was permanently ejected from paradise for this reason. Do you want to suffer the same fate as Satan? He thought that he was better than Adam (ﷺ) because he was made from fire, while Adam was made from clay. Realize that you are just like Satan when you think that you are better than someone else just because you have a slightly different melanin level or DNA sequence.

Read from the Qur'an every day, and reflect especially on the following verse:

《O mankind, indeed We have created you from male and female and made you peoples and tribes that you may know one another. Indeed, the most noble of you in the sight of Allah is the most righteous of you. Indeed, Allah is Knowing and Acquainted.》 *(Qur'an 49: 13)*

Reflect on these hadiths: «The Prophet (ﷺ) said (during his farewell sermon): O people, Remember that your Lord is One. An Arab has no superiority over a non-Arab, nor a non-Arab over an Arab; also a black person has no superiority over a white person, nor a white person over a black person, except by one's consciousness, awareness, respect, love, and fear of Allah (ﷺ). Indeed, the best among you is the one with the most consciousness, awareness, respect, love and fear of Allah. Listen to me. Did I convey this to you properly? People responded: Yes, O Messenger of Allah! The Prophet (ﷺ) then said: Then each one of you who is here must convey this to everyone who is not present.» (a sound hadith recorded by Bayhaqi)

The Prophet (ﷺ) said: «Let people stop boasting about their ancestors. One is only a pious believer or a miserable sinner. All men are sons of Adam (عليه السلام), and Adam came from dust.» (a sound hadith recorded by Abu Dâwood and at-Tirmidhi)

Reflect on the behaviour of the Prophet (ﷺ) and his Companion Abu Dharr (رضي الله عنه) in the following story. Narrated al-Ma'rur: «At ar-Rabadha, I met Abu Dharr, who was wearing a cloak, and his slave was wearing a similar one. I asked why, and he replied: I abused a person by calling his mother with bad names. The Prophet said to me: O Abu Dharr! Did you abuse him by calling his mother with bad names? You still have some characteristics of ignorance. Your slaves are your brothers, and Allah has put them under your command. So whoever has a brother under his command should feed him with what he eats and dress him with what he wears. Do not ask them (slaves) to do things beyond their capacity (power), and if you do so, then help them.» (Bukhari)

As far as actions are concerned, when you host an event or a meal, you should invite people from various races, ethnicities, and economic backgrounds. Honour those towards whom you feel arrogance, and make yourself humble by giving them places higher than your own place.

Begin doing things for yourself more, and have people serve you less. Become a servant of others, as our Prophet (ﷺ) was a servant of others. He (ﷺ) used to sew his own clothes, patch his own sandals and help his wives at home.

Devote yourself to finding the truth, regardless of where it comes from. Accept the truth whether it comes from a Muslim or a non-Muslim, a friend or an enemy, your religious scripture or a scientist, a Westerner or an Easterner, a man or a woman. Put your emotions aside and use reason. Study the principles of logical thinking, then apply them to your life.

At the time of the Prophet (ﷺ), many Arabs were prejudiced against black Africans, as was evident in the story of Abu Dharr (ﷺ), which was mentioned above. The Prophet (ﷺ) tried to combat this type of racism by marrying Arab women to black men, some of whom were of African descent. Notable examples are the marriage of Zaynab bint Jaḥsh to Zayd ibn al-Ḥârithah, Fâtimah bint Qays to 'Usâmah ibn Zayd, the daughter of 'Amr ibn al-Wahhâb to Sa'd al-Aswad (the last name is descriptive, meaning 'the black man'), and a woman of the *Anṣâr* [the inhabitants of Madinah who had accepted Islam and assisted the Prophet (ﷺ) and other emigrants upon their arrival there] to Julaybeeb.[11] Follow the example of the Prophet (ﷺ) and marry your daughters to men of the group towards which you feel arrogant (as long as they are pious, they have an equivalent income to you, and your daughters agree).[12]

When you find yourself making assumptions about people or stereotyping them, assume the opposite. Seek out people from that

---

[11] Imam Zaid Shakir, *Scattered Pictures: Reflections of an American Muslim* (Hayward, CA: Zaytuna Institute, 2005), 74-75. Shakir cites the following classical sources for these instances: aṭ-Ṭabari, *Jâmi' al-Bayân fee Ta'weel al-Qur'ân*, vol. 10, p. 301; Ibn al-Atheer, *Al-Kâmil fit-Târeekh [A Complete History]*, vol. 21, pp. 336-337; and Ibn Ḥajar al-'Asqalâni, *Fatḥ al-Bâri*, vol. 9, pp. 505-506.

[12] It is not advisable to marry your daughter to someone of a lower economic class, and this attitude is not arrogance. The reason it is not advisable is because she is used to a certain standard provided for by her father, so if her husband is not capable of providing the same standard for her, it could lead to a lot of marital problems. However, if the woman desires to marry a religiously suitable man, and her guardian agrees that he is religiously suitable, then there is nothing wrong with that, and they are fulfilling the Sunnah.

group who are the opposite of that stereotype and keep their company, until this idea is extinguished from your mind. For example, if you think that all people of a certain group are uneducated, then find people from that group who are highly educated, and take them as companions.

Greet Muslims of all ethnic groups with the Islamic greeting *as-salâmu 'alaykum* (peace be upon you). In fact, this is one of the prophetic cures for racism in Islam, and the Prophet (ﷺ) taught us in the authentic hadiths that it spreads love among the believers.

Abu Hurayrah (ﷺ) reported that the Messenger of Allah (ﷺ) observed: «By Him in Whose Hand is my life! You will not enter paradise until you believe, and you will not believe until you love one another. Shall I inform you of something by which, if you do it, you will love one another? Promote greetings amongst yourselves (by saying *as-salâmu 'alaykum*).» (Muslim)

I did not really understand how such a simple act could have such a great effect until I witnessed it myself. When I was in my early twenties, I knew a sister who demonstrated to me the effects of greeting with *as-salâmu 'alaykum* and not greeting with it. When sisters would greet her that way, she would love them and would be willing to do all types of charitable acts for them. When sisters of certain ethnic groups refused to greet her or to return her greeting, her heart would become filled with anger, resentment, hatred, and prejudice towards those sisters and their ethnic groups.

The more of the teachings of the Prophet Muhammad (ﷺ) you put into practice, the more you will witness these types of things. Those acts which we Muslims may deem small and insignificant can actually have huge effects. Simple acts such as greeting with *as-salâmu 'alaykum*, putting your foot next to the other person's foot when you stand in line for prayer, and not decorating copies of the

Qur'an[13] can actually avert disasters like Palestine and Kosovo. I know that sounds crazy, but when you start learning and practicing the Sunnah, you witness it and you know that it is true, even though it does not seem logical at first.

Stop using skin lightening cream. It is a major sin because you are changing the creation of Allah (ﷻ). Using this product has hidden shirk in it as well, because when you use it, you are unconsciously saying that Allah (ﷻ) did not do a good job when He created you the way that He did, and He says:

❨We have certainly created man in the best of stature❩ *(Qur'an 95: 4)*

According to a sound hadith narrated by 'Abdullah ibn Mas'ood (﵁), Prophet Muhammad (ﷺ) said: «Allah has cursed women who tattoo their bodies, wear false hair, pluck their eyebrows,[14] and artificially widen gaps between their teeth.[15]» (Bukhari and Muslim)

Realize that this idea of lightening your skin is from Satan, who says:

❨...and I will command them so they will change the creation of Allah.❩ *(Qur'an 4: 119)*

Listen to what everyone has to say, regardless of his or her background. Realize that the most knowledgeable person on earth can be wrong, while the most ignorant person can be right. Judge

---

[13] The Qur'an is meant to be read beautifully, but it should be in simple binding with simple pages. According to the authentic Sunnah, it should not be embellished with gold, ornamented, or decorated. The Prophet (ﷺ) warned us that doing so would lead to all types of problems in the Muslim world.

[14] Unless a woman's eyebrows are excessively thick

[15] Gaps between the front teeth were considered a sign of beauty in some cultures. [Editor]

each idea based on its supporting evidence, not by the person giving you the idea. Sometimes Allah chooses to communicate messages to us through the most unlikely people and from the strangest places. It may be Allah communicating a message to you through a person; He may be creating these words on this person's tongue and speaking to you through him or her. You may be rejecting the words of Allah (ﷻ) when you reject this person's idea.

Remember that you are human, and that all human beings are sinners (or were sinners at one time) who have faults. The person whom you are judging or looking down upon is better than you at some things and has strengths that you do not have. Likewise, you have faults and weaknesses that he or she does not have. Compare yourself to people (whether alive or dead) whom you see as better than yourself, and make every effort to be better. Never be satisfied with yourself, because no matter how good you are at something, there is always room for improvement. Always strive to be better, for as long as you live.

If you like to have people stand to greet you, and you get upset when they do not, then do not allow people to stand for you unless you are a guest in their homes.

If you are arrogant because of your strength and size, reflect on the fact that it is not an accomplishment of yours. Allah (ﷻ) gave you this strength and size, and He can take it away at any moment, with one accident or one illness. I experienced this personally when I was addicted to weightlifting about ten years ago and needed surgery. Before the operation, I was able to bench press about twice my body weight, but afterwards, even my own body weight felt heavy. I knew of someone else who was tall but then lost his legs; now he is no longer tall. Realize that your size and strength are gifts from Allah. Be grateful for them and use them for His sake. Realize that if you are arrogant, He may punish you in this life by taking away these gifts, but there may be a much worse punishment in the next life. Seek out people who are bigger and stronger than you, and keep their company.

Reflect on this hadith: «It is reported that 'Abdullah ibn Mas'ood (ﷺ) had thin, weak legs. Once, upon seeing his leg uncovered, some people laughed, whereupon the Messenger of Allah (ﷺ) said: Are you laughing at the frailty of his legs? By Him in Whose hand is my soul, on the scale of Allah, they are weightier than Mount Uhud.» (a reliable hadith recorded by Aḥmad and al-Tiyalisi)

Reflect on Allah's divine names ar-Razzâq (the Provider), al-Wahhâb (the Bestower), al-Mu'izz (the Bestower of Honour), ar-Râfi' (the Exalter), ar-Rabb (the Lord), and al-Wârith (the Inheritor). Realize that any wealth, power, intelligence or education that you have is a gift from Allah (ﷺ). Reflect on the lives of people who lost their wealth and power and who ended up dead, imprisoned, embarrassed, dishonoured or ashamed as a result. Think about the fact that they had money, power, prestige, intelligence and education because Allah (ﷺ) gave it to them, and they experienced poverty, powerlessness, shame, insanity or senility because Allah (ﷺ) took those things away from them. Acknowledge that everything you have is from Allah (ﷺ) and will be taken by Allah — either in this life or after your death, when He will inherit everything. Recognize that with more power, wealth, intelligence and education comes more responsibility and more accountability. The Qur'an states:

❨And know that your properties and your children are but a trial and that Allah has with Him a great reward.❩   *(Qur'an 8: 28)*

You have been given more by Allah (ﷺ), so more is expected of you. Call yourself to account before Allah calls you to account. Ask yourself if you are using your money, power, intelligence and education in the way that Allah (ﷺ) wants, or if you are using it in a way that Allah does not want. Call on Allah (ﷺ), using His divine names, to take these diseases away from you.

If you are arrogant with others whom you feel are not as beautiful as you, realize that they may have more internal beauty than you do. Spend time with people who are even more beautiful than you. Reflect on the fact that your beauty is only temporary and that in a few short years, you will no longer be beautiful. When that happens, do you want to be treated as you treat those whom you consider ugly?

Perhaps you feel superior to others because you believe that you have done more religious works or because you have committed fewer sins. Realize that the moment you feel proud of that, all of your good deeds may be nullified, while all of their good deeds may be accepted. Consider that Allah (﷾) may be causing them to sin or to do fewer works so that they stay humble and turn to him in repentance. Recognize that your life is not over yet, and neither is their life. You do not know where you will end up, and you do not know where they will end up. Reflect on the following hadiths:

«I swear by Allah — there is no God but He — that one of you may perform the deeds of the people of paradise until there is naught but an arm's length between him and it, when that which has been written will outstrip him so that he performs the deeds of the people of the hellfire; one of you may perform the deeds of the people of hellfire until there is naught but an arm's length between him and it, when that which has been written will overtake him so that he performs the deeds of the people of paradise and enters therein.» (Bukhari)

«Abu Hurayrah (﷠) said that the Prophet (ﷺ) was asked: Messenger of Allah! A certain woman prays in the night, fasts in the day, acts and gives charity, but injures her neighbours with her tongue. The Messenger of Allah (ﷺ) said: There is no good in her. She is one of the people of the fire. They said: Another woman prays the prescribed prayers and gives bits of curd as charity and does not injure anyone. The Messenger of Allah (ﷺ) said: She is one of the people of the garden.» (Bukhari)

Allah's Apostle (ﷺ) said: «A prostitute was forgiven by Allah (ﷺ) because when she passed by a panting dog near a well and saw that the dog was about to die of thirst, she took off her shoe and, tying it with her head cover, drew out some water for the dog. Allah forgave her because of that.» (Bukhari and Muslim)

Dressing nicely and questioning scholars is not arrogance

Dressing nicely is not in itself considered arrogance. As Muslims, we should be dignified. If Allah (ﷺ) made us wealthy, we should wear nice clothes and display His blessings with the intention of displaying our gratitude to Him. However, we should not dress to show off.

Some people state that it is arrogance to question a scholar and ask him for evidence. Actually, this is not the case; asking questions is part of seeking truth and seeking knowledge. If you wanted to, you could find some scholar somewhere who would say that almost everything you do is forbidden. Some go to extremes and make Islam too restrictive, while others go to the other extreme and make Islam a religion of amusement and play. Questioning is an honest person's way of seeking truth.

The argument that some use to say that one should not ask a scholar for evidence is the fact that the *tâbi'oon* (those who knew or met any of the Companions and transmitted hadiths from them) did not ask the Prophet's Companion Ibn 'Abbâs (ﷺ) for evidence. There are two reasons that this view is mistaken. First of all, one could point out that 'Umar ibn al-Khaṭṭâb (ﷺ) made Abu Moosâ al-'Ash'ari (ﷺ) bring a second witness to verify the hadith evidence that he brought: «'Ubayd ibn 'Umayr reported that Abu Moosâ sought permission from 'Umar (to enter the house) three times. Finding him busy (hearing no response), he left, whereupon 'Umar said (to the occupants of his house): Did you not hear the voice of 'Abdullah ibn Qays (the real name of Abu Moosâ al-'Ash'ari)? He was called back, and 'Umar asked: What prompted you to leave? Abu Moosâ replied: This is how we have been commanded to act. 'Umar said: Bring evidence (in support of it), otherwise I shall deal (strictly) with you. So Abu Moosâ set out and came to a group of the Anṣâr, and he asked them to bear witness before 'Umar about this. The Companions present there said: Even the youngest amongst us would bear out this fact. So Abu Sa'eed al-Khudri (who was the youngest one in that company, came to 'Umar and) said: We have been commanded to do so (when we visit the homes of other people). Thereupon 'Umar said: This command of Allah's Messenger (ﷺ) had remained hidden from me up until now due to (my) business in the market.» (Muslim)

In this case, 'Umar (ﷺ) did not just accept the ruling that Abu Moosâ al-'Ash'ari (ﷺ) mentioned; he made him bring proof.

The second reason that this argument is weak is that Ibn 'Abbâs (ﷺ) was especially known for his keen intelligence and his ability to memorize word-for-word, and in minute detail, what he heard and saw from the Messenger of Allah (ﷺ),[16] so the Companions had every reason to trust his word. Furthermore, Ibn 'Abbâs (ﷺ) learned directly from the Prophet (ﷺ) at a time before innovations had become widespread. Innovations and foreign cultures influenced the Islamic jurisprudence of the later generations, so one is not as safe with a modern day imam or scholar as they would have been with Ibn 'Abbâs (ﷺ).

---

[16] M. Khalid, *Men around the Messenger*, trans. M. Sharif (Beirut, Dar al-Kotob al-Ilmiyah, 2005).

Attachment to this world and not accepting death, greed, miserliness

One of the main goals in Islam, as well as in Buddhism and Christianity, is to become detached from the world and everything in it. In the Buddhist religion, the whole objective and philosophy is to detach oneself from all desires and not be attached to anything. According to the Christians' version of the Bible, Jesus (ﷺ) made his followers give up all of their material possessions to follow him; he went so far as to not permit one of his followers to bury his own father who had just died. Jesus (ﷺ) did not allow his followers to have any material possessions. To follow Christ, they had to sell all that they owned and give their money to the poor.

The Prophet Muhammad (ﷺ) also taught us to be detached, but in a much more balanced way. He (ﷺ) taught that we could become as wealthy as we want,[17] as long as the wealth is not what is in our hearts. Abu Hurayrah (ﷺ) narrated that the Prophet (ﷺ) said: «Being self-sufficient does not mean having a great amount of property, but being content with what one has.» (Bukhari and Muslim)

There are many ways to know if the *dunyâ* — the material world and its concerns — is in one's heart. If Allah (ﷺ) were to take away all a person's wealth and leave him or her impoverished, the one who had dunyâ in the heart would be devastated. He or she might become angry with Allah (ﷺ), curse Him and abandon worshipping Him because of this test from Him. On the other hand, one who did not have dunyâ in the heart might feel a sense of loss but could endure it patiently. He or she would realize that the wealth belongs to Allah, and that we just borrow it for a time. The true owner of the

---

[17] As long as the money is earned in a way that is permissible [Editor]

wealth, Allah (ﷻ), decided to take it back. Those who do not have dunyâ in their hearts realize that and do not let the loss bother them.

Another way to look at whether the dunyâ is in your heart is by examining how much time you spend in pursuit of it. For example, are you skipping the obligatory prayers due to work? At my job, the Muslims established congregational prayer, but one of the Muslims stopped praying with us. When I approached him, he said that his father had told him to stop praying at work because he did not want him to get fired. In fact, the man got fired that same year, while all of the other Muslims were still at the job six or seven years later. He was so afraid of losing his job that he disobeyed Allah (ﷻ), and Allah (ﷻ) took the job from him to teach him a lesson.

If you are working so much that you are neglecting the rights of your spouse, your children and yourself, then your heart is attached to pursuit of the dunyâ. Likewise, if you are making money by disobeying Allah (ﷻ), you are still attached to the dunyâ.

Of course, people can be attached to family members, friends, teachers, leaders, or other human beings. It is a natural human behaviour to cry when someone close to you dies; you spent years with that person, and you will miss him or her. The Prophet Muhammad (ﷺ) cried when his son Ibrahim (رضي الله عنه) died, according to hadiths collected by Bukhari. However, a true Muslim buries the individual and then moves on with his or her life, because the Muslim has dealt with and prepared for death. A Muslim realizes that Allah (ﷻ) gives us life when He chooses, and He takes it when He chooses. The Muslim accepts and submits to that. On the other hand, the person who has the spiritual disease of attachment is unable to let go of the deceased. He or she may wail over the grave, tear his or her clothes, scream, hyperventilate, become depressed or suicidal, rebel against the Creator, give up worship and/or turn to a life of disobedience.

People can also be attached to their ideas. They may have beliefs or ideas that they believe to be correct, and this is normal; however, a person of truth should not be attached to that opinion. The test comes when proof is brought that this idea is wrong. People of truth will accept the evidence, but those who are attached to their belief will cling to it despite the fact that it has been proven wrong.

To cure this disease, reflect on death and the purpose of life and death. Realize that death is the end of the body but not the soul. Reflect on the fact that life is short. Strive for quality and spiritual excellence in your life, and you will have a life of increasing fulfilment. Realize that the only things you can take with you when you die are your spiritual state and the effects of your good actions. Life is temporal; you — and everyone you know — are born to die. This life is not our end, but only a means to our end.

Reflect on Allah's name ar-Razzâq (the Provider) and on the certainty that whatever material possessions you acquire in this life, you were destined to get them. Reflect on Allah's names Mâlik al-Mulk (The Owner of All Sovereignty) and Thil-Jalâli wal-Ikrâm (Owner of Majesty and Honour). Realize that Allah (ﷻ) is the true owner of everything in His creation. In reality, we own nothing.

Strive for both spiritual excellence and material excellence, and inshallah He (ﷻ) will open both up for you. Give Allah (ﷻ) His rights, your job its rights, your family members their rights, and your body its rights, and you will have true success.

Give money regularly (monthly or weekly) to a charity or to the mosque.

Spend time around people who are generous and not materialistic, so that you pick up their characteristics.

Prepare for death. Follow the advice of 'Abdullah ibn 'Umar (ﺭﺿﻲ), who said: "In the evening, do not expect that you will live until the next morning, and in the morning, do not expect to live until the evening." (Bukhari)

Remember that the Prophet (ﷺ) said: «Take advantage of life before death (overtakes you).» (a sound hadith recorded by at-Tirmidhi)

Repent to Allah for your feelings of excessive attachment, and make supplications frequently for Allah to remove them from you.

Desiring esteem in the eyes of others

As a true believer in Allah (ﷻ), you should care about what Allah thinks of you, and not what others think. Being concerned about what others think of you is a disease of the heart. Most people are not truthful and sincere, so they cannot be pleased no matter what you do. Most people sit on the fence and follow leadership and popular opinion. If the leaders' opinion and popular opinion of you is high, they love you, but if those attitudes change, their opinion of you changes as well.

Follow the Sunnah and live according to the Sharia completely, and you will feel good about yourself when you go to bed each night, no matter what other people think of you. Reflect on the following verse of the Qur'an:

❴O you who have believed, enter into Islam completely [and perfectly] and do not follow the footsteps of Satan. Indeed, he is to you a clear enemy.❵   *(Qur'an 2: 208)*

You will feel at ease when you are facing Allah (ﷻ). When you abandon a Sunnah or a law of Sharia, you will not feel right with yourself when you sleep at night, and this will make you worry more about what people think.

If you find yourself concerned with what others think, evaluate yourself in all areas of your life. Start with the five pillars. Are you performing all of them? Do you give Muslims their rights? Do you give your families and your neighbours their rights? Do you give all people their rights? Study the laws of Sharia and apply them to your life.[18]

Next, look at the people whose opinions you care about. How does Allah (ﷻ) view them? You may admire their opinion, but Allah may despise them. Meditate on this fact regularly and think about it. If Allah (ﷻ) were to despise them on the Day of Judgment, would you want them to be pleased with you?

Continue to read your Qur'an in a language that you can understand. Reflect on the meaning of each verse and how it applies to your life intellectually, spiritually, and behaviourally. Read books on tawheed and ponder them. The reason you care about what others think is because your understanding of that concept is weak and/or you are not applying the Sharia in your life completely.

Worrying about what others think of you, even though you are doing the right thing, is blameworthy according to the Sharia. You should have consideration for other's feelings, because it is part of our religion to care about the feelings of others, but you should not compromise when it comes to following the Sharia. If Allah (ﷻ) says that something is obligatory, then you should do it regardless of what others think; conversely, if something is forbidden, you should not do it, regardless of what others think.

The rights due to Allah (ﷻ) take precedence over the rights of your parents, so if your parents try to get you to do something that goes against the Sharia, it is obligatory to disobey them. You should, however, try to kindly explain to them why you must disobey them in this matter. If that does not work, then ignore them from that point on

---

[18] A good book to start with is: Muhammad Subhi bin Hassan Hallaq, *Fiqh According to the Qur'an and Sunnah* (Riyadh: Dar-us-Salam Publications, 2007).

and do what Allah (ﷻ) says. It is commendable, though, to do extra acts of kindness towards people for the sake of Allah (ﷻ), expecting nothing in return. If you put your faith in Allah (ﷻ), you will never be disappointed, but if you put your hope in people, you will constantly be disappointed in life.

Repent for caring about what others think, and frequently make supplications for Allah to take this weakness out of your heart. Spend time with people who live their lives following the Sharia completely and who are not influenced by what others think.

Dishonesty

If you are dishonest with others, evaluate yourself and try to determine what is causing this. Is it because you are afraid of them? If so, then treat yourself for the disease of fearing other than Allah (ﷻ). Is it because you hope for things from them or desire things in their eyes? If the answer is yes, then treat yourself for the disease of desiring esteem in the eyes of others.

Are you dishonest with yourself? If this is the case, then treat yourself for the disease of attachment to the world (specifically the attachment to one's ideas). Ask others to evaluate you, and then listen to what they say. Repent sincerely for those things the people say about you, and make sincere supplications to Allah (ﷻ) to remove those faults from you.

Keep the company of sincere, honest people. Recite from the noble Qur'an daily.

Displeasure with the Decree of Allah

Ask yourself: are you all-knowing? Reflect on plans that you had that did not turn out the way you expected. What did you do wrong in those cases?

Reflect on Allah's divine names al-'Aleem (the Knowing), al-Khabeer (the Acquainted with all Things), al-Wâsi' (the All-Encompassing), and al-Ḥakeem (the Wise). Meditate on them and call on Allah (ﷻ) through His divine names, as the Qur'an teaches:

﴾And to Allah belong the best names, so invoke Him by them. And leave [the company of] those who practice deviation concerning His names. They will be recompensed for what they have been doing.﴿ *(Qur'an 7: 180)*

﴾Say: Call upon Allah or call upon the Most Merciful. Whichever [name] you call — to Him belong the best names. And do not recite [too] loudly in your prayer or [too] quietly but seek between that an [intermediate] way.﴿ *(Qur'an 17: 110)*

﴾He is Allah, the Creator, the Inventor, the Fashioner; to Him belong the best names. Whatever is in the heavens and earth is exalting Him. And He is the Exalted in Might, the Wise.﴿ *(Qur'an 59: 24)*

﴾Allah — there is no deity except Him. To Him belong the best names.﴿ *(Qur'an 20: 8)*

Repent sincerely to Allah (ﷻ), make sincere supplications and keep the company of those who do not suffer from this disease.

Recite from the noble Qur'an daily.

Not caring when you sin

Repent sincerely, supplicate to Allah and keep the company of those who fear Allah (ﷻ) and are conscious of Him and His laws most of the time.

Reflect on the following statements by the Companions of the Prophet (ﷺ). Anas ibn Mâlik (رضي الله عنه) said to one of his followers, "You imagine certain sins to be more insignificant than a hair, but at the time of the Prophet (ﷺ), we used to count them among those that can destroy a man." (Bukhari)

'Abdullah ibn Mas'ood (رضي الله عنه) said, "A believer treats a sin as if it is a mountain over his head that may fall on him any moment, whereas an immoral person looks at it as a fly that perched on his nose, which he waved away with his hand."[19]

Recite the Qur'an daily and reflect on what it says about the Companions of the Prophet (صلى الله عليه وسلم):

❰And the first forerunners [in the faith] among the Muhajireen[20] and the Anṣâr and those who followed them with good conduct — Allah is pleased with them and they are pleased with Him, and He has prepared for them gardens beneath which rivers flow, wherein they will abide forever. That is the great attainment.❱   *(Qur'an 9: 100)*

Reflect on the great rewards given to those who please Allah, the Exalted, Almighty.

Envy / jealousy / hatred of hearing praise for another person

Envy means wanting someone else to be deprived of a blessing that Allah (سبحانه وتعالى) gave them. Maybe you want it for yourself, or maybe you just do not want them to have it because you feel that they do not deserve it. This was the disease of Satan in the story of Adam (عليه السلام) and Satan, so reflect on this story.

Recite the Qur'an daily, and regularly recite the last three chapters of the Qur'an, especially soorat al-Falaq:

❰Say, 'I seek refuge in the Lord of daybreak from the evil of that which He created, and from the evil of darkness when it settles, and

---

[19] M. al-Munajjid, *I Want to Repent, But...* (Riyadh: International Islamic Publishing House, 2006), 12.

[20] Those who emigrated from Makkah and settled in Madinah for the cause of Islam

from the evil of the blowers in knots, and from the evil of an envier when he envies.'⟩   *(Qur'an 113: 1-5)*

In the last line, we are asking Allah (ﷻ) to protect us from the envious one as he envies. If we are the envious, we want Allah (ﷻ) to protect us from the evil in ourselves. Since the nature of Satan is that he is envious, we do not want him to inspire envy in us.

Reflect on the following hadith:

The Prophet (ﷺ) said: «None of you truly believes until he loves for (all) human beings what he loves for himself.» (Bukhari)

Start doing good deeds for the persons that you envy. Pray for them to have even more good things than they do now.

Repent for this disease, and make sincere supplications asking Allah (ﷻ) to remove it from your heart. Spend time with those who are generous, and constantly pray for others. Avoid the company of those who are envious, jealous, or full of hatred, and stay away from those who engage in backbiting.

Excessiveness

The Prophet (ﷺ) and his Companions (may Allah be pleased with them) were the perfect models of how to live and how to worship Allah (ﷻ) with moderation. Trying to outdo them in any category of behaviour is excessiveness. The cure for this is knowledge of the Sunnah and its implementation in your life. Constantly learn the Sunnah and put it into practice. The Prophet Muhammad (ﷺ) was the most humble of men, and his wives were the most humble of women. Learn humility from them, and do not go beyond that.

I used to teach Islamic jurisprudence to teenagers, most of whom were of a certain ethnic group. They had no knowledge whatsoever about *ghusl*, the ritual bathing that is considered a full purification; they did not know what it was or when it was required. It is recommended at certain times, including every Friday, and required at specific times, such as after sexual intercourse or after the completion of a menstrual period or postpartum bleeding. Their parents refused to teach them about it because it had to do with sex, and they felt too modest to talk about sex with their children. May Allah (ﷻ) destroy the innovation in their culture and remove it from them. In fact, the knowledge of ghusl is an obligation on every Muslim from the time he or she reaches puberty. The Prophet (ﷺ) used to discuss Islamic jurisprudence in regards to sex, even in the mosque, in the presence of children. Today's parents are not more modest than the Prophet (ﷺ) and his wives and Companions (may Allah be pleased with them). When they try to be more modest than them, their modesty becomes blameworthy and sinful.

Recite from the noble Qur'an daily.

Learn the Sunnah, learn the Sunnah, and learn the Sunnah. Implement the Sunnah, implement the Sunnah, and implement the Sunnah. Keep company with people who have knowledge of the Sunnah. Make supplications to Allah (ﷻ) to increase your knowledge and implementation of the Sunnah, and repent for the innovations that have crept into your knowledge and practice.

Reflect on the following hadiths:

«Anas (ﷺ) reported: Three men came to the houses of the wives of the Prophet (ﷺ) to inquire about the Prophet's (ﷺ) acts of worship. When they were informed, they considered their own worship insignificant and said: Where are we in comparison with the Prophet (ﷺ), while Allah has forgiven his past sins and future sins? One of them said: As for me, I shall offer prayer all night long. Another said: I shall observe fasting continuously and shall not break it. The other said: I shall abstain from women and shall never marry. The Prophet (ﷺ) came to them and said: Are you the people who said such and such things? By Allah, I fear Allah more than you do, and I am the most obedient and dutiful among you to Him, but still I observe fast and break it, perform prayer and sleep at night, and take wives. Whoever turns away from my Sunnah does not belong to me.» (Bukhari and Muslim)

Abu Hurayrah (رضي الله عنه) reported that the Prophet (ﷺ) said: «The religion is easy, and whoever makes the religion a rigour, it will overpower him. So follow a middle course (in worship). If you cannot do this, do something near to it, and give glad tidings and seek help (from Allah) in the morning and at dusk and in some part of night.» (Bukhari)

This should not be misinterpreted to mean that one should abandon obligatory duties if one finds them difficult. This specifically refers to voluntary acts, not mandatory ones.

«Anas (رضي الله عنه) reported that the Prophet (ﷺ) came into the mosque and noticed a rope stretched between two poles. He asked: What is this rope for? He was told: This is Zaynab's rope. When, during her voluntary prayer, she begins to feel tired, she grasps it for support. The Prophet (ﷺ) said: Untie it. You should perform prayers as long as you feel active. When you feel tired, you should go to sleep.» (Bukhari and Muslim)

«Abu Juhayfah (رضي الله عنه) reported that the Prophet (ﷺ) made a bond of brotherhood between Salmân and Abud-Dardâ'. Salmân paid a visit to Abud-Dardâ' and found the wife of Abud-Dardâ' dressed in shabby clothes, so he asked her why she was in that state. She replied: Your brother Abud-Dardâ' is not interested in (the luxuries of) this world. In the meantime, Abud-Dardâ' came in and prepared a meal for Salmân. Salmân requested Abud-Dardâ' to eat (with him), but Abud-Dardâ' said: I am fasting. Salmân said: I am not going to eat unless you eat, so Abud-Dardâ' ate (with Salmân). When it was night (and a part of the night had passed), Abud-Dardâ' got up (to offer the night prayer), but Salmân asked him to sleep, and Abud-Dardâ' slept.

After some time, Abud-Dardâ' again got up, but Salmân asked him to sleep. In the last hours of the night, Salmân asked him to get up, and both of them offered prayer. Then Salmân told Abud-Dardâ': You owe a duty to your Lord, you owe a duty to your body, you owe a duty to your family — so you should give everyone his due. Abud-Dardâ' came to the Prophet (ﷺ) and reported the whole story. Prophet (ﷺ) said: Salmân is right.» (Bukhari)

«'Abdullah ibn 'Amr ibn al-'Âṣ (رضي الله عنه) reported: The Prophet (ﷺ) was informed that I said that I would perform prayers the whole night and observe fasting every day as long as I live. The Messenger of Allah (ﷺ) said: Is it you who said this? I said to him: O Messenger of Allah! I ransom you with my parents; it is I who said that. The Messenger of Allah (ﷺ) said: You will not be able to do that. Observe fast and break it, sleep and get up for prayer, and observe fast for three days during the month; for every good is multiplied ten times, and that will be equal to fasting the whole year.» (Bukhari and Muslim)

«Ibn 'Abbâs (رضي الله عنه) reported that while the Prophet (ﷺ) was delivering a sermon, he noticed a man who was standing, so he asked about him and was told that he was Abu Isrâ'eel, who had taken a vow to remain standing and not to sit, go into the shade, or speak while fasting. Thereupon the Messenger of Allah (ﷺ) said: Tell him to speak, to go into the shade, to sit and to complete his fast.» (Bukhari)

'Â'ishah (رضي الله عنها) reported that the Messenger of Allah (ﷺ) said: «If anybody introduces a practice which is not authenticated by me, it is to be rejected.» (Muslim)

«Jâbir (رضي الله عنه) reported: When the Messenger of Allah (ﷺ) delivered the sermon, his eyes became red, his voice rose, and his anger increased so that he was like one giving a warning against the enemy and saying: The enemy has made a morning attack on you, and in the evening, too. He would also say: The last Hour and I have been sent like these two, and he would join his forefinger and middle finger. He would say: The best of the speech is embodied in the Book of Allah, and the best of guidance is the guidance given by Muhammad (ﷺ). The most evil affairs are their innovations, and every innovation is error. He would also say: I am, in respect of rights, nearer to every believer than his own self. He who leaves an estate, it belongs to his heirs, and he who leaves a debt, it is my responsibility to pay it off.» (Muslim)

Fear of other than Allah

Reflect on the following hadith: «Abu al-'Abbâs 'Abdullah ibn 'Abbâs (ﷺ) reported: One day I was behind the Prophet (ﷺ) (on a camel), and he said to me: O young man, I shall teach you some words (of advice): Be mindful of Allah (ﷺ), and Allah will be mindful of you. Be mindful of Allah, and you will find Him in front of you. If you (have need to) ask, ask of Allah; when you seek help, seek help from Allah. Know that even if the Ummah were to gather together to benefit you with something, they would not benefit you with anything except that which Allah (ﷺ) has already recorded for you. If they gathered together to harm you with something, they would not be able to harm you with anything except that which Allah (ﷺ) has already recorded against you. The pens have been lifted, and the pages have dried.» (a sound hadith recorded by at-Tirmidhi)

Reflect on the divine names al-Muhyee (the Giver of Life), al-Mumeet (the Giver of Death), and ar-Razzâq (the Provider), and meditate on them.

Recite from the Qur'an daily, and reflect on the following verse:

❴Wherever you may be, death will overtake you, even if you should be within towers of lofty construction.❵ *(Qur'an 4: 78)*

Repent and make supplications sincerely. Keep company with those who are courageous but balanced. Avoid the company of those who are foolishly courageous — those who take unnecessary risks and do not know when to walk away from a situation.

Gluttony

Reflect on the following hadiths:

Ibn 'Umar narrated that the Apostle of Allah (ﷺ) said: «A believer eats in one intestine (is satisfied with a little food), and a disbeliever or a hypocrite eats in seven intestines (eats too much).» (a sound hadith recorded by Ibn Mâjah and at-Tirmidhi)

On the authority of al-Miqdâm ibn Ma'di Karib (ﷺ), who said that he heard the Prophet (ﷺ) say: «No human ever filled a vessel worse than the stomach. Sufficient for any son of Adam are some morsels to keep his back straight, but if it must be, then one-third for his food, one-third for his drink and one-third for his breath.» (a sound hadith recorded by Aḥmad, at-Tirmidhi, an-Nasâ'i and Ibn Mâjah)

Practice fasting on Mondays and Thursdays and on the thirteenth, fourteenth and fifteenth days of every Islamic (lunar) month. After you have mastered the fasting, pick a healthy, balanced diet and stick to it.

Repent and make sincere supplications. Keep the company of those who eat moderately.

Recite from the noble Qur'an daily.

Hatred / Lack of compassion

In Islam, there are two concepts of hatred. One is forbidden, while the other is praiseworthy. The forbidden hatred is the type practiced by the Ku Klux Klan,[21] the Aryan Nations[22] and many terrorist groups run by satanic innovators who call themselves Muslims. This type of hatred is connected to envy, and it is a spiritual disease that is central to the story of Adam (ﷺ) and Satan. When you hate someone, you desire no good, and only harm, for that person. Sometimes you hate the person's very existence, which actually means that you hate the decree of Allah (ﷻ), and this is another spiritual disease. These types of hatred are against the spirit of Islam as reflected in the following hadith of the Prophet (ﷺ): «None of you truly believes until he loves for (all) human beings what he loves for himself.» (Bukhari)

Someone may ask, "What about all the verses that state that one should hate the disbelievers?" These verses exist and are true. However, what these verses mean by hate and what other people see as hate are two different things. This concept of hatred is better translated into English as disapproval, since we do not have the concept of praiseworthy hatred in our culture and language.

I will give a concrete example. I am Muslim, and my family is Christian. Some of them profess belief in the trinity, pray to Jesus (ﷺ) and to saints, and have paintings and graven images of what is supposed to be Jesus (ﷺ). Now, I can show them from their own Christian Bible where it says that these are the worse sins a human can commit. I can show them where their own Bible teaches that doing this is worse than murder, rape, genocide, or adultery — yet they still do this. I hate these beliefs and practices of theirs. However, since I still care for them, I want them to stop doing these actions and to accept Islam. I know how much of a difference Islam has made in

---

[21] A racist hate group that flourished in some parts of the U.S. south during the 19th and 20th centuries [Editor]

[22] A white nationalist neo-Nazi organization that was founded in the U.S. in the 1970s [Editor]

my life, and I want them to share in it with me. I love for them what I love for myself. If something makes me happy, I would love for them to share in it. I know that many of the issues with which they struggle would be solved by implementing the Sunnah.

This is the Muslim concept of hate. The English language does not have this concept of hate. I wish that translators would translate these verses and the various rulings about hating non-Muslims as disapproval, because the English language does not have this definition of hatred, even though the Arabic has both. The English definition is limited to the un-Islamic concept of hatred that I explained in the first paragraph of this section.

The Prophet (ﷺ) wanted his uncle, Abu Ṭâlib, to become Muslim because he cared about him; that is why he (ﷺ) was distressed when his uncle died a disbeliever. He did not want him to die a disbeliever because he (ﷺ) wanted the best for his non-Muslim uncle. Likewise, two of the greatest enemies of Islam at one time were Abu Jahl and 'Umar ibn al-Khaṭṭâb (ﺭﺿﻲ). The Prophet (ﷺ) wanted them to become Muslim, and he prayed to Allah (ﷻ) to strengthen Islam through one of them. 'Umar's (ﺭﺿﻲ) Islam was the fulfilment of that prayer.

If he (ﷺ) had hated them (according to the English definition of the word), he would never have wanted them to embrace Islam. He (ﷺ) would have been happy when Abu Ṭâlib died, and he would never have prayed for 'Umar ibn al-Khaṭṭâb (ﺭﺿﻲ) to become Muslim. He (ﷺ) would have hoped that 'Umar died a disbeliever. Instead, he (ﷺ) disapproved of their disbelief, but he had compassion for them as human beings. That is why he (ﷺ) prayed for them and hoped they would be guided. There is plenty of evidence in the Qur'an that the Prophet (ﷺ) was emotionally hurt because many of his people rejected Islam and remained polytheists.

If you have hatred in your heart — according to the English definition of the word — reflect on Allah's name al-Wadood (the Most Loving), and meditate on it. Also, reflect on the hadith mentioned previously: «None of you truly believes until he loves for (all) human beings what he loves for himself.» (Bukhari)

Repent sincerely and make sincere supplications to Allah (ﷻ) for this disease to be removed. Keep the company of those people who are very loving and compassionate. Do good deeds for the people you hate, and pray for them. Recite from the noble Qur'an daily.

Ignorance

The cure for ignorance is knowledge. However, when you study Islamic jurisprudence and Sharia, there is a hidden danger: You may begin to follow the letter of the law while neglecting the spirit of the law. To cure this, you must study *usool al-fiqh* — the study of how scholars derive the laws of Islam from the primary texts of the Qur'an and Sunnah — so you can begin to understand the purpose behind the laws. Also, learn about as many laws as you can, because they often have conditions and exceptions. If you are following the letter of the law when a condition or exception applies, you may actually be breaking the law itself. In addition, you should learn as many authentic hadiths as possible. As questions arise in your mind, and you begin to ask questions, your knowledge increases.

Make supplications to Allah (ﷻ) to give you knowledge and the wisdom to apply that knowledge correctly. Keep the company of scholars, so that your knowledge may increase.

Study the story of Jesus (عليه السلام), so that you can understand the danger of following the letter of the laws without following the spirit of those laws.

Reflect on the hadiths of the Prophet (ﷺ) that encourage one to seek knowledge.

Recite from the noble Qur'an daily.

Impatience

The cure for impatience is to reflect on the lives of people who live in conditions that are more difficult than yours. Study the Qur'an and the authentic biographies of the Prophet Muhammad (ﷺ). Read about all of the trials and the sufferings of the prophets (peace be upon them) and the Companions (may Allah be pleased with them) of the Prophet Muhammad (ﷺ). As you study their lives, take note of what they did during times of trial and hardship, and then follow their examples.

Using the supplications that the Prophet (ﷺ) used and taught, frequently ask Allah (ﷻ) to increase your patience in the way that is easiest for you.

Reflect on the promise of Allah (ﷻ) that He does not burden a soul with a burden greater than it can bear.

❨And do not approach the orphan's property except in a way that is best, until he reaches maturity. And give full measure and weight in justice. **We do not charge any soul except [with that within] its capacity**. And when you testify, be just, even if [it concerns] a near relative. And the covenant of Allah fulfil. This has He instructed you that you may remember.❩   *(Qur'an 6: 152)*

❨Whoever is guided is only guided for [the benefit of] his soul. And whoever errs only errs against it. **And no bearer of burdens will bear the burden of another**. And never would We punish until We sent a messenger.❩   *(Qur'an 17: 15)*

Realize that you can handle this trial; Allah (ﷻ) would not have given it to you otherwise. Remember that after every period of hardship comes a period of ease, and know that your situation will get better.

Recite from the noble Qur'an daily, and reflect on the following verses:

❲For indeed, with hardship [will be] ease. Indeed, with hardship [will be] ease.❳   *(Qur'an 94: 5-6)*

❲And He gave you from all you asked of Him. And if you should count the favours of Allah, you could not enumerate them. Indeed, mankind is [generally] most unjust and ungrateful.❳ *(Qur'an 14: 34)*

❲And Allah has extracted you from the wombs of your mothers not knowing a thing, and He made for you hearing and vision and intellect that perhaps you would be grateful.❳   *(Qur'an 16: 78)*

❲And whatever you have of favour — it is from Allah...❳
(Qur'an 16: 53)

❲And when My servants ask you, [O Muhammad], concerning Me — indeed I am near. I respond to the invocation of the supplicant when he calls upon Me. So let them respond to Me [by obedience] and believe in Me that they may be [rightly] guided.❳ *(Qur'an 2: 186)*

Reflect on all the hadiths of the Prophet (ﷺ) that teach the benefits of trials and tribulations.

Keep the company of those who suffer but display patience in their suffering. Keep the company of those who are worse off than you, so that you may become more appreciative of what you have.

Reflect on Allah's names aṣ-Ṣaboor (the Most Patient) and ash-Shakoor (the Appreciative), and call on Allah (ﷻ) by those names for help.

Each day, get out a piece of paper and write down everything that you have to be grateful for in life, and then thank Allah (ﷻ) for each of those things.

Also, thank people for all they have done for you. Abu Hurayrah (عنه الله رضي) narrated that the Messenger of Allah (ﷺ) said: «He who does not thank people, does not thank Allah.» (a sound hadith recorded by Aḥmad and at-Tirmidhi)

Ingratitude

Read the section on impatience, and follow the advice in that section.

Gratitude to Allah (ﷻ) is mainly shown through fulfilling our obligations towards Him. Everything good in our lives is from Allah (ﷻ); therefore, He deserves more of our gratitude than anyone or anything else. He gives us everything and asks for very little in return. Below is a list of things that we owe to Allah (ﷻ) in return for all that He does for us.

❖ to worship Him alone and not ascribe partners to Him[23]

❖ to pray only to Him, fast only for Him and offer sacrifices only to Him[24]

❖ to perform the five daily prayers

❖ to fast the month of Ramadan (unless there is a legal Sharia excuse)

❖ to perform *hajj* (the pilgrimage to Makkah) once in our lifetime, if we are physically and financially able

---

[23] «Mu'âdh ibn Jabal (عنه الله رضي) relates that the Prophet (ﷺ) said to him: O Mu'âdh! Do you know what is Allah's right over His servants and what their right is over Him? I said: Allah and His Messenger know best. He said: Allah's right over His servants is that they worship Him without associating any partner with Him in worship, and their right over Him is that He does not punish anyone who worships Him without associating any partner with Him in worship.» (Bukhari and Muslim)

[24] The Prophet (ﷺ) said: «Islam is built upon five (pillars): the testimony that there is no god but Allah and that Muhammad is the Messenger of Allah;=

❖ to abstain from committing major sins[25]

❖ to strive to abstain from committing minor sins

❖ to repent for our wrong actions

❖ to strive to purify our hearts from spiritual diseases

If you fulfil your obligations towards Allah (ﷻ), you will have a happy and fulfilling life. If you do not fulfil these obligations, your soul and conscience will never be totally at peace. You will go to an extreme in one or more of these spiritual diseases, if not all of them. The Prophet (ﷺ) taught that your insides will become dark: «When the servant performs a sin, a black spot appears on his heart. If he seeks forgiveness, this black spot is removed, and if he returns to sin, the black spot grows until his heart becomes black. This is the stain about which Allah spoke: ﴾No! Rather the stain has covered their hearts of that which they were earning.﴿ *(Qur'an 83: 14)*» (a reliable hadith recorded by an-Nasâ'i and at-Tirmidhi)

Recite from the noble Qur'an daily.

Injustice

Learn the Sharia and follow it, whether it is in your favour or against you, whether it is in support of or against your family. Do what is right, regardless of what others say.

=establishing regular prayer; paying the zakâh; hajj (pilgrimage) and fasting Ramadan.» (Bukhari)

[25] «It was narrated on the authority of Abi Tha'labah al-Khushâni Jurthum ibn Nasheer (﵁) that the Messenger of Allah (ﷺ) said: Verily Allah the Almighty has prescribed the obligatory deeds, so do not neglect them; He has set certain limits, so do not go beyond them; He has forbidden certain things, so do not indulge in them; and He has said nothing about certain things, as an act of mercy to you, not out of forgetfulness, so do not go enquiring into these.» (a reliable hadith recorded by Dâraqutni)

Frequently reflect on the Prophet's statement that he would cut off the hand of his own daughter Fâṭimah (﷽) if she were guilty of stealing. Reflect on the incident during the caliphate of 'Umar ibn al-Khaṭṭâb (﷽) when 'Umar's son Abu Shaḥmah was found guilty of drinking alcohol in Egypt. Abu Shaḥmah insisted on being lashed as anyone else would be. When 'Umar (﷽) found out, he had him sent back to Madinah, where he flogged his son again in a show of fatherly discipline.[26] Reflect on the hadiths that warn of the serious consequences of being unjust, an oppressor, or a tyrant.

Repent sincerely for this shortcoming of yours, and supplicate to Allah (﷽) to remove this from you.

Keep the company of people whom you know are just and who almost always do the right thing, no matter what the consequences.

Read the section on the disease of desiring esteem in the eyes of others, and follow the advice in that section.

Recite from the noble Qur'an daily.

Insincerity

If you feel that you are not sincere in your actions, then choose good actions that you dislike, from which you expect no worldly benefit, and do them for the sake of Allah (﷽).

Fast for the sake of Allah. «Abu Hurayrah (﷽) reported that the Messenger of Allah (﷽) said: Allah (﷽) said: Every act of the son of Adam is for him, except the fasting, which is (exclusively) for Me, and I will reward him for it. Fasting is a shield. When any one of you is observing fast, he should neither indulge in obscene language

---

[26] A month later, Abu Shaḥmah became sick and died. He did not die as a result of the flogging, as some have claimed.

nor should he raise his voice; if anyone reviles him or tries to quarrel with him, he should say: I am fasting. By Him in Whose Hand the soul of Muhammad is, the breath of one fasting is sweeter to Allah than the fragrance of musk. The one who fasts experiences two joys: he feels pleasure when he breaks the fast, and he is joyful by virtue of his fast when he meets his Lord.» (Bukhari and Muslim)

Frequently make supplications to Allah (ﷻ) to purify your intention. Repent. Keep the company of people who outwardly demonstrate signs of piety and sincerity. Recite from the noble Qur'an daily.

Judging others

Create a list of your sins and bad qualities. At the end of each day, write down the sins that you committed, and repent for each one.

Realize that while you are judging others for some shortcoming, you have that fault inside yourself, even if you do not recognize it or believe that you have it. Usually, when we really dislike something about a person, it is an issue with which our own subconscious is struggling. As a human being, each of us has the potential to commit every evil and every good action on earth. When you understand that, you will be less judgmental of others.

Read the section on arrogance, and follow the advice in that section. Recite from the Qur'an daily.

Lack of consideration for others

Frequently read stories that demonstrate the good character of the Prophet (ﷺ), until they melt and soften your heart. Study the Sharia and try to implement it in your life.

Repent sincerely and make frequent supplications to Allah (ﷻ) asking Him to remove this character flaw from you.

Keep the company of those who are considerate and who display exemplary character.

Recite from the noble Qur'an daily.

Lack of discipline / laziness

The remedy for this one has to come from inside you. Practice Islam, because Islam creates discipline. Follow the advice in this book. In this instance, follow the slogan of the sportswear company Nike: 'Just Do It'. If your parents did not instill discipline in you, it is time for you to take responsibility for yourself and discipline yourself — no matter how hard that may be.

Repent sincerely and make frequent supplications to Allah (ﷻ), asking Him to remove that character flaw from you. Keep the company of those who have discipline, and follow them. Make the specific supplications of the Prophet (ﷺ) to remove laziness. Recite from the noble Qur'an daily.

Love of leadership / power

Read the section on desiring esteem in the eyes of others, and follow the recommendations found there. Reflect on the following hadiths:

'Abdur-Rahmân ibn Samoorah (﵁) reported that the Messenger of Allah (ﷺ) said to him: «Do not ask for a position of authority.[27] If you are granted this position without asking for it, you

---

[27] There is an exception to this rule. If you know that you are the most qualified and that there is no one else qualified to do the job, it is not blameworthy to seek leadership in that case, because not seeking leadership could be more harmful to the people. However, you should check your ego and hate the position. If someone better comes along, you should step down and relinquish the position for the sake of Allah (ﷻ).

will be helped (by Allah) in discharging its responsibilities; but if you are given it as a result of your request, you will be left alone as its captive...» (Bukhari and Muslim)

The Prophet (ﷺ) said: «I swear by Allah! We do not give this leadership to anyone who seeks it or is greedy for it.» (Bukhari)

Abu Hurayrah (ﷺ) reported that the Messenger of Allah (ﷺ) said: «You will covet getting a position of authority, but remember that it will be a cause of humiliation and remorse on the Day of Resurrection.» (Bukhari)

«Abu Moosâ al-Ash'ari (ﷺ) reported: I called on the Prophet (ﷺ) with two of my cousins. One of them said to him: O Messenger of Allah (ﷺ), appoint me governor of some land over which Allah has given you authority. The other also requested something of the same nature. The Messenger of Allah (ﷺ) said: By Allah, we do not appoint to this post someone who seeks it or someone who contends for it.» (Bukhari and Muslim)

«Abu Maryam al-Azdi (ﷺ) reported: When I entered upon Mu'âwiyah (ﷺ), he said: How good your visit is to us, O father of so-and-so. (This is an idiom used by the Arabs on such occasions). I said: I will tell you a hadith that I heard (from the Prophet). I heard the Messenger of Allah (ﷺ) say: If Allah puts anyone in a position of authority over the affairs of the Muslims, and he secludes himself (from them), not fulfilling their needs, wants, and poverty, Allah (ﷺ) will keep Himself away from him, not fulfilling his needs, want and poverty. He said: He (Mu'âwiyah) appointed a man to fulfil the needs of the people.» (a reliable hadith recorded by Abu Dâwood and at-Tirmidhi)

Abu Ya'lâ Ma'qeel ibn Yâssar (ﷺ) reported that the Messenger of Allah (ﷺ) said: «Any slave whom Allah puts in charge of subjects, and who dies while he is not sincere to them, Allah will make paradise unlawful for him.» (Bukhari and Muslim)

Allah's Messenger (ﷺ) said: «He who does not look after his subjects with goodwill and sincerity will be deprived of the fragrance of paradise.» (Bukhari and Muslim)

The Messenger of Allah (ﷺ) said: «A ruler who, having control over the affairs of the Muslims, does not strive diligently for their betterment and does not serve them sincerely, will not enter paradise with them.» (Muslim)

Ibn 'Umar (ﷺ) reported that the Messenger of Allah (ﷺ) said: «Surely! Every one of you is a guardian and is responsible for his charges: The imam (ruler) of the people is a guardian and is responsible for his subjects; a man is the guardian of his family (household) and is responsible for his subjects; a woman is the guardian of her husband's home and of his children and is responsible for them; and the slave of a man is a guardian of his master's property and is responsible for it. Surely, every one of you is a guardian and responsible for his charges.» (Bukhari and Muslim)

'Â'ishah (ﷺ) reported that she heard the Messenger of Allah (ﷺ) supplicating in her house: «O Allah! Treat harshly those who rule over my Ummah with harshness, and treat gently those who rule over my Ummah with gentleness.» (Muslim)

«'Awf ibn Mâlik (ﷺ) reported that the Messenger of Allah (ﷺ) said: The best of your rulers[28] are those whom you love and who

---

[28] This refers to a caliph, king, president, dictator or the like. The Prophet (ﷺ) declared: «This affair began with prophethood and as a mercy; then it will be mercy and caliphate; afterwards it will change into a cruel monarchy, and finally into iniquity and tyranny.» (a sound hadith recorded by Bayhaqi)

He (ﷺ) also prophesied: «Surely, the caliphate after me will last thirty years (which is how long it was before Ḥasan ibn 'Ali surrendered the caliphate); afterwards it will be a cruel monarchy.» (a reliable hadith recorded by Aḥmad and at-Tirmidhi) Even though the leaders of the Muslims until 1921 were called caliphs, they were kings or tyrants (except a few), according to=

love you, and those who supplicate to Allah (ﷻ) in your favour, and for whom you supplicate to Allah in their favour. The worst of your rulers are those whom you hate and who hate you, whom you curse and who curse you. It was asked (by those who were present): Should we not oppose them? He (ﷺ) said: No, as long as they establish the prayer; as long as they establish prayer in your midst.» (Muslim)

Ibn 'Umar (﵁) reported that the Prophet (ﷺ) said: «It is obligatory upon a Muslim to listen (to the ruler) and obey whether he likes it or not, except when he is ordered to do a sinful thing; in such a case, there is no obligation to listen or to obey.» (Bukhari and Muslim)

«Wa'il ibn Ḥujr (﵁) reported that Salamah ibn Yazeed al-Ju'f (﵁) asked the Messenger of Allah (ﷺ): O Prophet of Allah! Tell us, what do you command us to do if there arise over us rulers who demand of us what is due to them and refuse to give us what is due to us? The Messenger of Allah (ﷺ) turned away from him, but he repeated the same question. Thereupon Messenger of Allah (ﷺ) said:

=the definition of the Prophet Muhammad (ﷺ). The Prophet (ﷺ) forbade overthrowing any ruler of a Muslim country (or non-Muslim ruler, for that matter), no matter how tyrannical they are and how many blatant sins they commit, as long as they pray. Revolutions are not permissible in Islam. The reason for this is that (most of the time) more people die and are harmed in a revolution than through living under a tyrant. In another authentic hadith, the Prophet (ﷺ) stated that if he were to live to see the revolutionaries and terrorists (Kharijites), he would destroy all of them the way the people of 'Âd were completely destroyed. Even if a Muslim ruler in a Muslim country abandons the prayer, the Muslims have to look at whether they have the ability to overthrow that Muslim ruler and whether overthrowing him would cause less harm than leaving him in power. They are only allowed to overthrow a Muslim ruler who abandons the prayer if they have the capability and if removing the ruler will not cause greater harm to the people living there than leaving him in power would.

Listen to them and obey them. They are responsible for their obligations, and you are accountable for yours.» (Muslim)

Abu Hurayrah (رضي الله عنه) reported that the Prophet (ﷺ) said: «Seven are (the persons) to whom Allah (ﷻ) will give protection with His shade, on the day when there will be no shade except His (on the Day of Resurrection). They are: A just ruler; a youth who grew up with the worship of Allah; a person whose heart is attached to the mosque; two persons who love and meet each other and depart from each other for the sake of Allah; a man who is seduced (for illicit relations) by a beautiful and high ranking woman, but who rejects this offer by saying: I fear Allah; a person who gives charity and conceals it (to such an extent) that the left hand might not know what the right has given; and a person who remembers Allah in solitude and his eyes well up.» (Bukhari and Muslim)

'Iyad ibn Himar (رضي الله عنه) reported that the Messenger of Allah (ﷺ) said: «The people of paradise will be of three kinds: A just successful ruler, a man who shows mercy to his relatives and a pious believer who has a large family and refrains from begging.» (Muslim)

Reflect on the fact that the Companions (may Allah be pleased with them) did not seek leadership, and that many of the great imams of Islam ran away from leadership positions. As a leader, you will be accountable for any harm that you do to people. The harm that you cause can affect thousands, millions or billions of people, and it can affect generations. The Companions (رضي الله عنهم) did not seek leadership because they did not want that accountability on the Day of Judgment. It is hard enough being a parent, because you are responsible for your children. As a leader, you are responsible for everyone you lead and for the effects of your decisions on those whom you lead.

Recite from the noble Qur'an daily.

Procrastination

The key to stopping procrastination is setting up a schedule for your life. Modern scientific research shows that those who write down their schedules and post them in their houses are more likely to follow through than those who do not. When you make this schedule, start with the obligations; write down all of them, and do them first. Pray each of the five daily prayers as soon as the time comes. Make sure that you fulfil all of your daily obligations; when they are finished, then do what you like.

If you work with deadlines, then make your own personal deadline, which should be half of your actual deadline, and stick to it. That frees up the rest of the time for yourself and reduces stress in your life. Instead of doing a great deal of the work in one day — the last day — set aside a specific amount of time each day for working on the project, and then do a little bit each day.

As with all other spiritual diseases, procrastination requires that you repent sincerely and make sincere supplications, keep the company of those whose characteristics are the opposite of the disease that you are trying to defeat, and recite from the noble Qur'an daily.

Selfishness

Human beings are innately selfish. Being selfish is the way we survived as infants; when we were hungry, we cried and woke our parents so that we could eat. We did not consider that since Mommy and Daddy were sleeping, we should not disturb them; we selfishly woke them up. If we humans did not have this characteristic, we would not survive. However, when we continue to practice this as adults, at the expense of others, it becomes harmful.

Follow the advice in the sections on attachment to the world, greed, hatred, and lack of consideration for others. Recite from the noble Qur'an daily.

Shirk

Shirk, or associating partners with Allah, is a proof that you do not sincerely believe in One God, no matter what you may say. There are three types of shirk: shirk in recognizing Allah (﷼) as Lord, shirk in Allah's names and attributes, and shirk in the worship of Allah (﷼).

Monotheists believe that Allah (﷼) is in control of everything. Everything that is going to happen to us has already been decreed by Allah (﷼) and happens by His will and His power. Only Allah (﷼) has true power over everything. Only He can help or harm; only He (﷼) can give life or cause death.

Some Muslims commit shirk in this area by believing that an object can bring good luck or bad luck. Some non-Muslims do this by knocking on wood. They believe that the wood can protect them from harm, while in reality it is only Allah (﷼) that can help or harm. Knocking on wood only makes one farther from Allah instead of closer. Other Muslims believe that groups such as the Jews, the Freemasons,[29] the Americans, the Illuminati,[30] the United Nations and the like are in control of everything and cause everything that happens in the world. These people have committed shirk, since it is only Allah (﷼) who controls everything. Some Muslims commit shirk by reading and believing in horoscopes. This is shirk in Allah's

---

[29] A fraternal organization, established several hundred years ago, which has millions of members around the world today [Editor]

[30] A secret society believed by some to control events around the world, with the purpose of establishing a New World Order [Editor]

lordship, since horoscopes teach that the position of the stars is controlling what happens in your life, while in reality it is Allah (ﷻ) who is in control.

Monotheists also pray only to Allah (ﷻ) and ask for help only from Allah, as we say every day when reciting soorat al-Fâtiḥah, the first chapter of the Qur'an, in prayer:

❨You [Alone] we worship, and you [Alone] we ask for help [for each and every thing].❩   *(Qur'an 1: 5)*

However, some Muslims commit shirk by praying to the dead or by traveling to the graves of dead Muslims and asking them for help. This is shirk in worship. Others practice sorcery or magic, or call for help from the *jinn*, who are non-human, rational beings created by Allah from fire, often referred to as 'demons' or 'devils'. Some people try to 'foretell' the future by contacting jinn, and some disobedient jinn mislead people into thinking that they can tell them what will happen in the near or distant future, or that the jinn can provide people with riches or some sort of power. This is also shirk, since it involves calling on other than Allah (ﷻ), from amongst the unseen.

Additionally, monotheists believe that Allah's rules are better than any other rules. Some Muslims commit shirk by believing that the rules of their culture are superior to the rules of Allah (ﷻ). For example, if you bring a verse of Qur'an or an authentic hadith to these people and prove to them that they are incorrect from the viewpoint of the Sharia, they say, "But in my country, we do it this way," or "But this is against our customs." Thus, they have made their cultures and customs partners with Allah (ﷻ); in fact, they have even raised them above Allah (ﷻ).

The cure for shirk is to read the Qur'an in your own language. Reflect on what each verse reveals about who Allah (ﷻ) is and how

He wants you to live, and apply each verse to your life. In particular, reflect on the following verses, and act upon them:

⁅Indeed, Allah does not forgive association with Him, but He forgives what is less than that for whom He wills. And he who associates others with Allah has certainly fabricated a tremendous sin.³¹⁆   *(Qur'an 4: 48)*

⁅If you invoke them, they do not hear your supplication; and if they heard, they would not respond to you. And on the Day of Resurrection they will deny your association.⁆   *(Qur'an 35: 14)*

⁅And it was already revealed to you and to those before you that if you should associate [anything] with Allah, your work would surely become worthless, and you would surely be among the losers.⁆
                                                              (Qur'an 39: 65)

⁅O people, an example is presented, so listen to it. Indeed, those you invoke besides Allah will never create [as much as] a fly, even if they gathered together for that purpose. And if the fly should steal a [tiny] thing from them, they could not recover it from him. Weak are the pursuer and pursued.⁆   *(Qur'an 22: 73)*

⁅And those they invoke other than Allah create nothing, and they [themselves] are created.⁆   *(Qur'an 16: 20)*

⁅And they worship other than Allah that which neither harms them nor benefits them, and they say: These are our intercessors with Allah. Say: Do you inform Allah of something He does not know in

---

³¹ This is qualified by other verses, such as ⁅...And never would We punish until We sent a messenger.⁆ *(Qur'an 17: 15)* Once a person has had shirk explained to them and they continue to commit it, it is an unforgivable sin. If they are ignorant, we leave it up to Allah (ﷻ) to judge their hearts on the Day of Judgment. Also, if one repents from shirk and embraces Islamic monotheism, the previous shirk is forgiven.

the heavens or on the earth? Exalted is He and high above what they associate with Him.❭　　　　　　　　　　　*(Qur'an 10: 18)*

❰Indeed, Allah does not forgive association with Him, but He forgives what is less than that for whom He wills. And he who associates others with Allah has certainly gone far astray.❭

(Qur'an 4: 116)

❰Do they associate with Him those who create nothing and they are [themselves] created? And the false deities are unable to [give] them help, nor can they help themselves.❭　　*(Qur'an 7: 191-192)*

Reflect on the Prophet's (ﷺ) saying: «Whoever dies while still invoking other than Allah (ﷻ) as a rival to Allah will enter the Fire.» (Bukhari)

Read books on Islamic monotheism and apply them to your life.

Showing off in good works

Read the sections on arrogance and desiring esteem in the eyes of others, and follow the advice therein.

Reflect on the fact that by showing off, you nullify your good deeds and turn them into evil deeds. Would you show off your sin? When you show off your good works, you are in fact showing off your sins. Reflect on the fact that you just may have done this 'good work' for nothing because of your showing off.

Recite from the noble Qur'an daily.

Suspicion and not giving people the benefit of the doubt

Recite from the noble Qur'an daily, and reflect on this verse of the Qur'an:

❨O you who have believed, avoid much [negative] assumption. Indeed, some assumption is sin. And do not spy or backbite each other. Would one of you like to eat the flesh of his brother when dead? You would detest it. And fear Allah; indeed, Allah is Accepting of repentance and Merciful.❩   *(Qur'an 49: 12)*

Reflect on these hadiths: «Abu Hurayrah (ﷺ) reported that the Messenger of Allah (ﷺ) said: Beware of suspicion, for suspicion is the greatest falsehood. Do not try to find fault with each other, do not spy on one another, do not vie with one another, do not envy one another, do not be angry with one another, do not turn away from one another, and be servants of Allah (ﷺ), brothers to one another.» (Bukhari and Muslim)

Ibn 'Umar (ﷺ) narrated that the Messenger of Allah (ﷺ) said: «O you who declare Islam with your tongues but whose hearts have not been reached by faith, do not annoy the Muslims nor seek out their faults, for he who seeks out the faults of his brother Muslim will have his faults sought out by Allah (ﷺ), and when Allah (ﷺ) seeks out someone's faults, He exposes them, even if he is in the interior of his house.» (Bukhari and Muslim)

As with all other spiritual diseases, you need to repent sincerely, make sincere supplications and keep the company of those who have the opposite characteristic of the disease you are trying to defeat.

Avoiding suspicion and not giving people the benefit of the doubt has more to do with the state of your tongue than the state of your heart. Allah (ﷺ) communicates to us through our intuition. For example, you may get a bad feeling inside about someone when it comes to your children. You can act on that intuition and not let your children near that person when you are not present. However, you cannot say that that person is a kidnapper, molester, or anything else because you have no proof. You did not witness him doing anything, and you are not even entirely sure whether your feeling is accurate.

Wastefulness

Recite from the noble Qur'an daily, and reflect on this verse:

❨Indeed, the wasteful are brothers of the devils, and ever has Satan been to his Lord ungrateful.❩   *(Qur'an 17: 27)*

Reflect on the following hadiths, and act accordingly. Al-Mugheerah ibn Shu'bah (رضي الله عنه) reported that Allah's Messenger (ﷺ) said: «Verily Allah, the Glorious and Majestic, has forbidden for you: disobedience to mothers, burying daughters alive, withholding the right of others in spite of being able to return that to them and demanding that (which is not one's legitimate right). He disapproved three things for you: idle talk, persistent questioning and wasting of wealth.» (Muslim)

«Anas (رضي الله عنه) said: The Prophet (ﷺ) ordered us not to leave anything on the plate, and he said: You do not know in which portion of your food Allah has put the blessing.» (Muslim)

Imam Mâlik (رحمه الله) once said that if you have to sell something on behalf of another person, you can, but then when you hand over the money, you must advise him or her to use it wisely and to take care of it. If the person then starts to waste that money, or use it in bad ways, you can stop him or her from doing that, because the Prophet (ﷺ) forbade wasting property.

«Narrated Ibn 'Umar (رضي الله عنه): A man was often cheated in buying. The Prophet (ﷺ) said to him: When you buy something, say (to the seller): No cheating. The man used to say it from that time forward.» (Bukhari)

The Struggles of the Unmarried and the Married

$\mathcal{T}$his chapter is lengthy, but it is extremely important. It addresses some of the most critical issues faced by young Muslims, especially in the West, where they are trying to resist a culture that promotes sex everywhere. Their struggle is made more difficult by the fact that many of their parents have left the Sunnah when it comes to these matters, and many do not even have a clear understanding of what the Sunnah has to say on this topic. The ignorance of many of the Muslims on these issues is leading to a worsening of these problems. After reading this chapter, inshallah, Muslims will have clarity on the following issues and will be able to resolve them, in many cases.

❖ how the Sharia controls the sex drive and prevents sex outside marriage

❖ what a teen should do if his/her sex drive is out of control, how to approach parents, what to do if the parents refuse to follow the Sharia

❖ what if I am under eighteen in the United States, or my suitor cannot financially provide for me?

❖ what can parents do in this society to get their children married without them being harmed financially?

❖ the difference between natural sexual desire, which is part of our innate human nature and is embraced by Islam, and the spiritual disease of lust

❖ the signs that one has the spiritual disease of lust, as opposed to the natural sexual desires, and what to do if that is the case

❖ the number one solution for lust in Islam is marriage, with proofs from the Sunnah

❖ the obligations of both spouses towards Allah (ﷻ)

❖ the obligations of the husband and wife towards each other

❖ the causes of marital problems and their remedies

❖ the Islamic rulings on polygyny, and the reasons for polygyny

❖ Divorce in the eyes of the Sunnah and the way of our predecessors, versus the way of 'culture'

❖ the recommended time for marriage, according to the Sunnah

❖ the legal rulings concerning marriage, and when marriage becomes an obligation

❖ the purpose of marriage according to the Sunnah, versus the purpose of marriage in your 'culture'

❖ why men (and women) turn to pornography, Internet chat rooms, 'cybersex' and the like, and how implementing the Sunnah can prevent that

❖ the nature of men and women as explained by the Qur'an, Sunnah, and modern science

❖ the step-by-step process that an abused woman should take to attain her Islamic right to be protected, if her husband is threatening her safety

In Islam, sexual desire in itself is not viewed as a spiritual disease, as it is in Buddhism and Christianity. (There is a difference between the natural God-given sexual desire and the spiritual disease called lust, as we will explain throughout this section.) The ideal in Buddhism and Christianity is to be celibate and to free oneself from sexual desire altogether, but the fact is that if celibacy were practiced completely, it would lead to our extinction. Since the objective of Sharia (divine laws) is to preserve the souls and lives of humanity, celibacy has to be against the law of Allah (ﷻ).

The sex drives of many men and women are highest during their teenage years. According to Sharia, it can either be obligatory or recommended for men and women to get married in their teenage years. Once the sex drive begins to become strong, men and women are supposed to be married.

It is my opinion that parents should begin looking for spouses for their children by the age of sixteen. If daughters or sons come to their parents and tell them that they need to get married because they are struggling to control their sexual desires, then it becomes **obligatory** for the father or guardian to begin searching for a husband or wife for that young person. Shaykh Fawzan states in *A Summary of Islamic Jurisprudence, Volume 2*:

> Marriage becomes **obligatory** for those who fear committing *zinâ* (adultery or fornication), as marriage is a means of chastity and avoidance of what is prohibited... They also maintain that in this case, one's financial state does not matter. Shaykh Taqiyyud-Din said: "According to the apparent view of Aḥmad, as well as the majority of scholars, one should not consider wealth before marriage, as Allah, the Exalted be He, says, ❴...**If they should be poor, Allah will enrich them from His bounty...**❵ *(Qur'an 24: 32)* Even the Messenger of Allah (ﷺ) sometimes had nothing in his house as well. He (ﷺ) once concluded marriage for a man who could not even afford a ring of iron (as a dowry)."

This poses a problem in the United States of America and other Western countries, where many parents have embraced filthy, disgusting innovations. One of these is refusing to get their children married when they are sexually ready and trying to force them to wait. Another innovation is regarding a young woman as immodest or a whore for having a sex drive and wanting to have it satisfied. The truth is that Allah (ﷺ) created her with this sex drive. It is from her *fiṭrah*, the natural inclination of humans instilled by Allah; it is part of her being a normal, healthy functioning human being. May Allah (ﷻ) guide the innovators and destroy their innovations from amongst us.

My sex drive is out of control. What should I do?

Step 1 — Approach your father or guardian and tell him, no matter how challenging that may be for you. If he is a true Muslim, he will understand and do what he is supposed to do — get you married. If he refuses, he may just be ignorant of the Sharia.

Step 2 — If this is the case, speak to an imam, or another upright Muslim man[32] in your community, who knows and follows the correct interpretation of Islamic law regarding marriage, according to the Sunnah and the Sharia, and who does not follow the rules and misinterpretations of any particular culture. If he is willing to stand up for what is right and help you, then let him act as an arbitrator. Have him approach your father or guardian with the proofs from the Qur'an and Sunnah. If your father is a true Muslim, he will submit to the laws of Allah, since a Muslim by definition is one who submits to Allah (ﷻ). Then you can be married inshallah.

If your father still refuses, he is either a weak Muslim or one who is spreading corruption throughout the earth, whether he realizes it or not.

The Prophet (ﷺ) said: «If someone comes to you whose piety and character you are satisfied with, marry (an eligible female) to him. If you do not do so, there will be trials on the earth and a great deal of evil (or 'you will spread trials and corruption throughout the earth').» (a reliable hadith recorded by at-Tirmidhi)

---

[32] In the traditional Muslim world, one could go to a judge, but we do not have this position in the U.S.

Some argue that this hadith is only a recommendation. This opinion is incorrect on the basis of the Qur'an and Sunnah, because if a Muslim sees corruption and has the ability to change it, he or she must change it. The following verses and hadiths prove this:

❨And let there be [arising] from you a nation inviting to [all that is] good, enjoining what is right and forbidding what is wrong, and those will be the successful.❩   *(Qur'an 3: 104)*

❨The believing men and believing women are allies of one another. They enjoin what is right and forbid what is wrong and establish prayer and give zakâh and obey Allah and His Messenger. Those — Allah will have mercy upon them. Indeed, Allah is Exalted in Might and Wise.❩   *(Qur'an 9: 71)*

❨You are the best nation produced [as an example] for mankind. You enjoin what is right and forbid what is wrong and believe in Allah. If only the People of the Scripture had believed, it would have been better for them. Among them are believers, but most of them are defiantly disobedient.❩   *(Qur'an 3: 110)*

The Prophet (ﷺ) said: «Whoever among you sees something abominable should rectify it with his hand; if he has not strength enough to do that, then he should speak against it; if he has not strength enough to do that (even), then he should (abhor it) in his heart, and that is the least of faith.» (Muslim)

Also, it is forbidden for a Muslim to spread corruption. The hadith quoted previously states that one who refuses to marry his daughter to a suitable man, for a reason that is not valid under the Sharia, is actually spreading corruption (or tribulations) throughout the earth.

We see this happening all over the West. Muslim youths feel their hormones starting to rage, so they ask to be married, but their parents tell them that they cannot get married until they are in their twenties or thirties. Then the young Muslim sneaks off (sometimes even climbing out of a window) with another Muslim, or a non-Muslim, and goes to a private place to commit fornication. Before long, fornication and adultery become rampant. All this occurs because fathers refuse to marry their daughters to suitable matches for other than a Sharia reason. If this continues, the Muslim community will be plagued just like the non-Muslim community, as the Prophet (ﷺ) stated in an authentic hadith:

«'Abdullah ibn 'Umar (ﷺ) narrated: The Prophet (ﷺ) came to us and said, 'O Emigrants, you may be afflicted by five things; Allah (ﷻ) forbid that you should live to see them. If zinâ (fornication, adultery, homosexuality, and the like) should become widespread, you should realize that this has never happened without new diseases, which their ancestors never suffered, befalling the people. If people should begin to cheat in weighing out goods (in business), you should realize that this has never happened without drought and famine befalling the people, and their rulers oppressing them. If people should withhold *zakâh* (obligatory charity), you should realize that this has never happened without the rain being stopped from falling; were it not for the animals' sake, it would never rain again. If people should break their covenant with Allah (ﷻ) and His Messenger (ﷺ), you should realize that this has never happened without Allah sending an enemy against them to take some of their possessions by force. If the leaders do not govern according to the Book of Allah, you should realize that this has never happened without Allah (ﷻ) making them into groups and making them fight one another.» (a reliable hadith recorded by Ibn Mâjah and al-Hâkim)

Step 3 — If your father or guardian still refuses to accept the proofs from the Qur'an and Sunnah, then your arbitrator should approach your father's father with the proofs. If that does not work, the arbitrator should speak to other adult males in your family, in this order: your brother, then your father's brother, then the son of your father's brother, then any male relative from your father's side. Hopefully, someone in the line will be a true Muslim and submit to the laws of Allah (ﷻ) and marry you to a pious Muslim of good character and equal economic standing. If all of the people in your line refuse, then an imam or appointed arbitrator must take the responsibility himself and arrange for you to be married.

The same process should be taken when a father refuses suitors solely on the basis of race or ethnicity. In this case, the arbitrator should ask the father why he refused the man. If the father says that it was a matter of deen and character, while the daughter disputes that, then the arbitrator himself should investigate the character and religion of the suitor by going to family members, teachers, neighbours, friends, co-workers, and associates of the suitor. If the father is correct about the character and religion of the man, then the woman is forbidden to marry him. If it turns out that the father is lying, then the arbitrator/imam should continue with steps 1 to 3, as described above.

I was blessed to take personal classes in uṣool al-fiqh with Shaykh Muhammad Qatanani, who had dealt with this issue. A man approached him, wanting to marry a woman who was from a different background than him. The shaykh knew that her family was not a pious family, so he discouraged the man and told him to think about it more. The man came back saying that he had to marry her because he feared that they would engage in pre-marital sex. However, the woman's father said no, because this man was American and a convert to Islam, while their family was from a different country, and their ancestors were Muslim. Shaykh Qatanani married them because the father did not have a valid, Sharia reason to prevent them from marrying. The Shaykh explained that, according to the Sharia, if the judge investigates and does not find anything wrong with the religious practice or character of the man, then he can act as her *wali*[33] and marry the couple.

On the other hand, there was an instance where another brother approached Shaykh Qatanani. In this case, the woman's father had not refused; he simply had not decided yet because he was still in the process of investigating the man, which was his responsibility. The shaykh stated that he would not marry this couple because the father had a legitimate Sharia reason.

What if I am under the age of consent or my suitor cannot provide for me financially?

Only steps 1 and 2 apply to you. If your father says no, make supplications and go to the mosque frequently. Fast on Mondays and Thursdays each week, as well as the thirteenth, fourteenth and fifteenth days of each lunar month. If this still does not work, observe the fast of David (ﷺ), which means fasting on alternate days.

What can parents in this society do to help their children get married without causing them financial harm?

Some parents do not want their children committing fornication and sincerely wish to help them, but they also realize that their sons are not in a position to financially provide for a family. What can they do?

These parents may have to consider nontraditional options. They could let the young person marry and then bring his or her spouse to live with them in the parents' home (which is traditional in some parts of the world), or they could let the couple marry but continue to live separately, each with his or her own parents. If pregnancy is not desirable during this time, there are various methods

---

[33] The wali is the woman's guardian, usually her closest male relative on her father's side. He plays an important role in looking out for her interests and finding a suitable husband for her. [Editor]

of birth control available, including implants that are effective for up to three years.

What are the rights and responsibilities of the woman and the wali?

If Muslims complied with these guidelines, most of these problems would be avoided. The daughter has the right to marry a suitable match when she can no longer wait to be married or is struggling to preserve her chastity. The role of the wali is to find her a suitable match, consistent with the Sharia, and to prevent her from marrying someone who is not appropriate. A suitable match is someone who is her equal in religion, character and economic position. A wali can reject someone who is not religious or who has bad character, and he can turn down someone who makes less money than the woman does (although he does not have to if he thinks they are a good match otherwise). The woman is obliged to accept the wali's judgment in this case. He does not have the right to decline a suitor for other than these three reasons. If the father is refusing suitable matches for other reasons, the daughter then has the right to appeal to a judge (or in a non-Muslim country, an arbitrator) to examine the situation. If the judge determines that the father is preventing his daughter from marrying a suitable match for a reason that is against the Sharia, he should go through the multi-step process that we discussed earlier.

The role of the wali is to protect the young lady in accordance with the Sharia, not to harm her by following innovations. The Prophet (ﷺ) was fair and protected the rights of both the wali and the woman. Unfortunately, too many so-called Muslims have adopted innovations in the religion that have stripped young ladies of the rights that Allah (ﷻ) gave them. Sadly, very few Muslims will stand up and confront these innovations that permeate our communities.

How the sharia controls the sex drive and prevents extramarital sex

Islam, Judaism and Christianity all teach that sex outside of marriage is a major sin. This is not as difficult for Muslims and Jews from practicing religious families, because we have preventions and alternatives. Many Christians and Westerners find it almost impossible to comply with this prohibition, though, because they lack the preventions of the Sunnah.

The primary prevention is marriage, as I emphasized previously. The Qur'an also tells us to lower our gaze.

❨Say to the believing men that they should lower their gaze and guard their modesty; that will make for greater purity for them, and Allah is well acquainted with all that they do. And say to the believing women that they should lower their gaze and guard their modesty; that they should not display their beauty and ornaments except what [must ordinarily] appear thereof; that they should draw their veils over their bosoms and not display their beauty except to their husbands, their fathers, their husband's fathers, their sons, their husbands' sons, their brothers or their brothers' sons, or their sisters' sons, or their women, or the slaves whom their right hands possess, or male servants free of physical needs, or small children who have no sense of the shame of sex; and that they should not strike their feet in order to draw attention to their hidden ornaments. And O ye believers! Turn ye all together towards Allah, that ye may attain bliss.❩[34]   (*Qur'an 24: 30-31*)

The Prophet (ﷺ) advised 'Ali ibn Abu Ṭâlib (ﷺ): «'Ali, do not let a second look follow the first. The first look is allowed to you

---

[34] This translation of the meaning is taken from Ali, *The Glorious Qur'an: Translation and Commentary.*

but not the second.» (a reliable hadith recorded by Aḥmad, Abu Dâwood and at-Tirmidhi)

Next, Islam requires both men and women to wear loose clothing that covers their bodies and conceals the shapes of most people. If everyone dresses in this way, people are less likely to become sexually excited by seeing the average man or woman walking down the street. Dressing modestly makes it easier for men and women not to be enticed into pre-marital and extra-marital sex.

The Prophet Muhammad (ﷺ) taught that a man and woman who are not married to each other, but who are not *mahram* (in other words, a man and woman who are eligible for marriage to each other) are not allowed to be in a room alone together. This principle also should be applied to phone calls and Internet chat rooms, because the Prophet also said: «The fornication of the eyes is to look with lust; the fornication of the tongue is to speak lustful things; the fornication of the hands is to touch with lust; the fornication of the feet is to walk towards lust; the fornication of the heart is to desire evil.» (Bukhari and Muslim)

The Prophet (ﷺ) said: «A man and a woman are never alone together, except Satan is their third.» (a sound hadith recorded by Ibn Mâjah)

There are many reasons for this. First of all, if a man and woman are not in a room alone together, they are less likely to be tempted into having sex outside of marriage. Secondly, if a woman is alone with a man, there is a higher chance of her being raped or sexually assaulted; avoiding this will result in a decline in the number of rapes and sexual assaults. Third, there will be fewer rumors spread among members of the community, because if a man and woman are alone together and are seen, people might talk; this talk can turn into rumors and can damage reputations. We see this all the time in American tabloids; a man is photographed alone with a woman, and articles about their affair are published in magazines that are displayed at the front counter of grocery stores. If the two were alone together, they have no alibi.

Lastly, Islam limits the mixing between men and women. We do not sit together in mosques, and for the most part, we do not talk to one another unless we are co-workers, family members, or friends of our spouses or family. The Companions (may Allah be pleased with them) did not go to the extreme of seclusion or never speaking to members of the opposite sex, as many Muslims do today; nor did they go to the extreme of constant mixing, as many non-Muslims do.

What if I follow the sharia and still cannot control my sex drive?

First, let us review all of the following Sharia techniques:

1. marriage
2. daily sexual intercourse with one's spouse
3. lowering the gaze
4. dressing in modest clothing
5. avoiding seclusion (including one-on-one phone calls and chatting) with members of the opposite sex who are not mahram
6. limiting contact with members of the opposite sex who are not mahram
7. voluntary fasting on Mondays and Thursdays and on the thirteenth, fourteenth and fifteenth days of every Islamic (lunar) month (except on days when fasting is prohibited, like the days of *Eid*)
8. voluntary fasting on alternate days (except during Ramadan and on days on which fasting is prohibited, like the Eid celebrations)

Signs that you have the spiritual disease of lust

We explained previously that Islam does not see sexuality as a disease, but instead as a part of our nature that should be embraced.

However, if you are doing all that the Sharia says, and your sexual craving is not satisfied, then you have the spiritual disease of excessive lust. If you have this disease, you might be in danger of committing one or more of the sexual acts that the Sharia considers unlawful. Even if you do not commit them, you will have a strong urge in your heart to do so. It will be stronger than a passing, evil thought, since an evil thought will repulse you, making you seek refuge with Allah (ﷻ) and implore His divine forgiveness. The disease will manifest itself by becoming a pleasurable desire that you crave (even if you do not act upon it).

If you have tried all the things in the Sharia, and these desires are still plaguing you, then you must repent and make supplications frequently, especially at the best times. Keep the company of pious Muslims who do not occupy themselves by thinking or talking about these things. When the evil thoughts come to your mind, stand up, face Makkah, and start reciting as much as you are able to recite of the Qur'an. This should calm the heart and repel the thoughts. If this still does not work, then you may want to consider moving to a Muslim country where most of the people in the area are practicing Islam.

In the true Islam (not the innovations that some Muslims call their 'culture'), sexuality is embraced. We embrace our sexual desire and try to fulfil it to the utmost extent within the boundaries of marriage. According to Islam, the main purpose behind marriage is to allow two people to have lawful sexual intercourse. The Arabic word that is used for marriage, *nikah*, can also refer to sex. So in one sense, in the Islamic religion, marriage and sex are equivalent. The purpose of marriage in Islam is to preserve one's chastity by having a lawful partner for sex. This leads to procreation and an environment where children can then be nurtured to maturity.

There are many proofs of this in the authentic Sunnah. First, let us examine the rights and responsibilities of the husband and wife in marriage. The primary obligation of the wife is to make herself sexually available to her husband. All scholars of Islam agree on this, while there is some disagreement on other obligations. For example, some scholars say that a woman has an obligation to cook, while others say that she does not; both opinions have their proofs from the Qur'an and Sunnah. According to the Sharia of Islam, the woman who does nothing all day but pleases her husband sexually when he comes home from work is better than the woman who cooks, cleans, and contributes to the household financially, but does not make herself available when her husband needs her sexually.

This does not mean that the main value of a woman is her sexuality. Rather, this is because it is possible for a man to have all of his other needs met by someone other than his wife, while his sexual needs can only be lawfully satisfied by her. Likewise, a woman's sexual needs can only be lawfully satisfied by her husband.

Marriage

Obligations towards one's wife

In Islam, a man's main responsibility is to provide the woman with the five things listed below.[35]

1. housing equivalent to what her father provided for her[36]

---

[35] The man must provide financial support for his wives and children and sometimes to other female relatives. The wife and children have a right to part of the husband's money, while the husband has no right to any of his wife's money. A woman's money is solely hers, and she has no financial responsibility for anyone. This explains why under Islamic Law, in most cases, the woman's share of an inheritance is half that of the man's.

[36] This has two conditions. First, her father must have provided for her from a lawful source and without using interest to acquire these things. Secondly, if the woman knew that the man could not provide equivalent housing and married him anyway, then she has to accept that she consciously chose to=

2. one new outfit (dress, shoes, coat, gloves, scarf, veil and so on) in the winter and one new outfit in the summer, of equal quality to what her father provided for her

3. sufficient food for her to stay healthy and not go hungry,[37] in accordance with the level of food provided for her by her father[38]

4. products she needs to beautify herself for her husband (such as soaps, deodorants, what she needs to get her hair done, and anything that he would like to see her wear)

5. physical security

Women were created weaker than men physically, whether the so-called modern woman likes it or not. The average woman has less upper body strength than the average male and cannot physically withstand an attack from a man. She is also held back from the same level of career advancement due to pregnancy and childrearing. At the same time, women were given strengths that men were not given; for example, the average woman is more merciful, modest, and well behaved than the average man.

What the majority of women seek in a relationship is security, both economic and physical. Although many women today can work to support themselves, they still desire these things from a man, even if it is unconsciously.[39]

=marry a man who could not provide for her in the same way her father did.

[37] If the husband and wife are impoverished, they may still be hungry. In this case, one needs enough food to ensure survival.

[38] However, if her family were gluttons and did not follow the Sharia in their eating habits, you do not have to feed her on the same level in which her father fed her. Instead, she should be fed with the same quality food that her father fed her with, but according to the quantities designated by the Sharia: one-third of the stomach for food, one-third for drink, and one-third for air.

[39] There are books on the market that explain how men can seduce and succeed with women, and the methods in these books work with the vast=

Kind treatment — Respecting her, speaking to her nicely, showing her love and forgiveness

Anthropological studies have shown that there are few things that are common to every culture in the world. Some of them are: the belief in the supernatural, the institution of marriage, the recognition that incest is wrong, the males being more aggressive from childhood, and the fact that women are more obedient from childhood. In Islam, we would say that these things are part of our fiṭrah, which is the inherent nature that all human beings have. The Prophet (ﷺ) said: «Every child is born on fiṭrah, then his parents make him a Jew, Christian, or a Zoroastrian.» (Bukhari)

The nature of the woman is to be obedient. Despite the views of many women who have been raised on American television, obedience is not a bad thing, except in certain instances (such as obeying someone like Adolf Hitler). In American public schools, girls are better students than boys, in general. Girls are more likely to complete their class work and homework, and they are less likely to talk back to teachers in a discourteous manner. On average, girls get better grades in American schools than boys, because they are more obedient to their teachers and less likely to rebel.

However, as Allah (ﷻ) informed us in the Qur'an and Sunnah, human beings are capable of changing the fiṭrah. In cases where women do not feel physically safe, provided for financially, or treated with love and kindness and respect, they act against their

---

=majority of women. I can tell you from personal experience, because I have tried them myself as an experiment. I was successful when I did exactly what the books told me, and I was unsuccessful when I did exactly what the books told me not to do. All of these subconscious techniques work on career-oriented, independent women as well, because they take advantage of human nature — even if expressing the realities of human nature is politically incorrect in modern times.

nature. We see this quite often in the public housing projects in the U.S., where many young ladies grow up without physical and economic security and without being treated with respect. They often take on the characteristics of men, because they are forced into situations where they have to defend themselves, both verbally and physically. In many cases, they also have to provide financial support for their households. For these reasons, many young women act against their fiṭrah, becoming rebellious and aggressive in response to a tough environment that does not foster or nurture that natural inclination.

If a woman is lacking kindness, love, respect and self-worth at home, this will affect the household, the community, and even the world. When women are not treated with kindness and love, they may seek it from somewhere else. Poor treatment also can affect their relationship with Allah (ﷻ) and can lead them into sins. In the worst cases, they may leave Islam or commit adultery with someone who speaks to them nicely. Clearly, women are responsible for their own actions and will be fully accountable before Allah (ﷻ) for what they do; however, husbands are partially accountable for any sins that their wives commit in reaction to, or as a result of, poor treatment from their husbands.

'Abdullah (ﷺ) narrated that the Prophet (ﷺ) said: «No human being is killed unjustly, but a part of responsibility for the crime is laid on the first son of Adam who invented the tradition of killing (murdering) on the earth.» (Bukhari)

Ibn 'Umar (ﷺ) narrated from his father (ﷺ) that the Prophet (ﷺ) said: «The deceased is tortured in his grave for the wailing done over him.» (Bukhari and Muslim)

It may seem that the previous two hadiths contradict this verse of Qur'an:

❴... And no bearer of burdens will bear the burden of another...❵
(Qur'an 17: 15)

However, when you understand the explanation of these hadiths, you can see the divine harmony between the Qur'anic verse and the hadiths. The reason the man is being punished in the grave for his widow's action is because she was under his care, and it was his responsibility as a Muslim husband to correct her and educate her. He neglected this duty, and that is why she was wailing over his grave. Her action was a result of his action.

You are partially responsible for the actions of those under your care, which is another reason why many of the Companions (may Allah be pleased with them) did not want to be rulers. They knew that for every misstep they took that was followed by someone else, or that resulted in someone else's sin, they would be held accountable to some degree. Imagine being accountable for the actions of hundreds of thousands of people. The historian Ali M. Sallâbi, in his biography of the second caliph 'Umar ibn al-Khaṭṭâb (ﷺ), wrote, "He regarded his caliphate as a trial with which he was being tested and for which he would be brought to account as to whether he had done his duty properly."[40] For this reason, people feared leadership; however, when leadership was thrust on someone like 'Umar (ﷺ), he stepped up to the task. He did not evade his responsibility or run away from it, as would many who go to extremes in fear of leadership.

A man's lack of kind treatment towards his wife can affect the community and the world in many ways. For one thing, victims of abuse often turn around and abuse others who are seen as less powerful. For example, let us say that a man abuses a woman who is a member of the same ethnic group. This woman then goes to the

---

[40] Ali M. Sallâbi, *'Umar ibn al-Khattâb: His Life and Times*, (Riyadh: International Islamic Publishing House), 175.

mosque, where the majority of women are from her ethnic group, but there are also minorities from two other ethnic groups. The woman knows that the women from these minority ethnic groups are weaker in the community, so she takes her frustrations out on them and shows them no kindness. As a result, they may stop going to that mosque and may harbor prejudice towards her ethnic group. Then they pass that prejudice on to other people. In the worst case, they might leave Islam. The mosque now loses membership and money. Groups or individuals stop feeling spiritually secure and become susceptible to committing more sins because they do not frequent the mosques as often.

Likewise, if the parents teach their children that it is acceptable to mistreat others, then those children may go to school and abuse other students, who in turn treat others badly. Eventually, they may grow up and mistreat their spouses, and the cycle repeats itself.

All of the above things could happen because of what a husband saw as a simple action or a small sin — mistreating his wife.

On the other hand, if one does a good deed and teaches or influences others in the process, he or she receives a reward for everyone who is affected, until the Day of Judgment. For example, every time I perform the ritual prayer, I get a reward inshallah. Ramazan Zuberi gets a reward inshallah. Brother Yaqub gets a reward inshallah. Bilal Philips gets a reward inshallah. Imam al-Bukhari gets a reward inshallah. The hadith narrators get a reward inshallah. The Prophet Muhammad (ﷺ) gets a reward inshallah... and countless others, whom I do not even know, get rewards because they taught someone, who taught someone else, who eventually taught me. This is why we can never match the Companions of the Prophet (may Allah be pleased with them). For every good deed we do, they are also getting rewards because we could not do the good deeds in the first place if it were not for them. This is why the Prophet Muhammad (ﷺ) will get the greatest reward on the Day of Judgment and will receive the highest place in paradise. He has more followers, who do more good deeds, than any of the prophets (peace be upon them) who came before him.

The Messenger of Allah (ﷺ) said: «Nations were displayed before me; one or two prophets would pass by, along with a few followers. A prophet would pass by accompanied by no one. Then a big crowd of people passed in front of me, and I asked: Who are they? Are they my followers? It was said: No, it is Moses (عليه السلام) and his followers. It was said to me: Look at the horizon. Behold! There was a multitude of people filling the horizon. Then it was said to me: Look there and there about the stretching sky! Behold! There was a multitude filling the horizon. It was said to me: This is your nation, out of whom seventy thousand shall enter paradise without reckoning...» (Bukhari)

Abu Hurayrah (رضي الله عنه) narrated that the Prophet (ﷺ) said: «There was no prophet among the prophets who was not given miracles because of which people had security or had belief, but what I was given was the divine inspiration that Allah revealed to me. So I hope that my followers will be more than those of any other prophet on the Day of Resurrection.» (Bukhari and Muslim)

Abu Mas'ood 'Uqbah ibn 'Amr al-Anṣâri al-Badri (رضي الله عنه) reported that the Messenger of Allah (ﷺ) said: «Whoever guides someone to virtue will receive a reward equivalent to him who practices that good action.» (Muslim)

Abu Hurayrah (رضي الله عنه) reported that the Messenger of Allah (ﷺ) said: «If anyone calls others to follow right guidance, his reward will be equivalent to those who follow him (in righteousness) without their reward being diminished in any respect, and if anyone invites others to follow error, the sin will be equivalent to that of the people who follow him (in sinfulness) without their sins being diminished in any respect.» (Muslim)

Fulfilment of her sexual needs

According to the Sunnah, the woman has a right to be sexually fulfilled. The husband who does not fulfil his wife's sexual needs and desires may be driving her to commit adultery; if she does that, she is fully accountable in this world and in the next, but he is also partially accountable in the next world inshallah. There are some deviant cultures, calling themselves Muslim cultures, which teach that a woman should not initiate sex and should just wait for her husband to do so. This is nonsense; may Allah (ﷻ) destroy these innovations and remove them from amongst us. *Âmeen* (amen). Both the man and the woman have the right to be fulfilled, and either one may make the first move. Both the men and women from amongst the Companions (may Allah be pleased with them) used to initiate sex.

The woman has a greater sexual capacity than a man, and the only thing that prevents women from using this more than men do is the intense modesty that Allah gave them as part of their innate human nature.[41] Modern science has verified that the average woman is able to have more, longer and more intense orgasms than a man can. In this sense, men are actually sexually inferior to women. Despite that, in the majority of cultures of the world, men are polygynous (able to have more than one wife at a time); according to anthropologist Helen Fisher in her work *Anatomy of Love*, eighty-four percent of the world's cultures are polygynous. There are only two or three cultures in the world that are polyandrous (where women have more than one husband at a time).

---

[41] A man has a higher sex drive, and that is why he is by nature polygynous. A woman is more naturally monogamous; however, she has a greater capacity to enjoy sex with that one man. This is why many women can naturally have multiple orgasms, and much longer and more powerful orgasms, than men. Most women can also engage in sex for a longer period of time than most men can.

In her well-known book *Brain Sex,* geneticist Anne Moir verified Helen Fisher's anthropological conclusions that men are by nature polygynous and women are by nature monogamous. Almost everywhere in the world, men have more sexual partners than women do, despite the fact that they are sexually inferior to women. The reason for this is that women were made more modest as part of their fiṭrah.

In American culture, where premarital sex is encouraged, one still sees remnants of this. From the time a boy is about twelve years old, he is ready for sex. If an attractive girl tries to seduce a boy, it is almost unheard of for a boy (or a man) say, "I'm not ready yet," or "It just doesn't feel right." He is ready to lose his virginity at the first opportunity. On the other hand, it may take a girl a while to feel physically and/or emotionally ready for sex. Many girls feel uncomfortable for a little while when they lose their virginity. This still occurs among many adult women who may have had over a dozen sexual partners. No matter how attractive a man is physically, he has to make her 'feel' that she wants to have sex with him. An average man, on the other hand, only has to look at a woman, and if she is sexually attractive, he will be ready to have sexual intercourse with her.

The Prophet Muhammad (ﷺ) gave the husbands of the Ummah advice on how to make love to the wives of the Ummah, and he gave Muslims, in general, a lot of sex education. «Abu Dharr (ﷺ) reported that some of the Companions (may Allah be pleased with them) of the Messenger of Allah (ﷺ) said to him: O Messenger of Allah, the rich have taken away all the rewards. They observe the prayer as we do, and they keep the fasts as we do, and they give charity from their surplus riches. Upon this, he (ﷺ) said: Has Allah not prescribed for you (a course) to follow, by which you can also do charity? Verily every (time you say) *subḥânallâh* (glory be to Allah) there is a charity, every (time you say) *Allâhu Akbar* (Allah is the

Greatest) is a charity, every (time you say) *alḥamdulillâh* (all praise is for Allah) is a charity, every (time you say) *lâ ilâha illâ Allâh* (there is none worthy of worship other than Allah) is a charity, enjoining of good is a charity, forbidding of evil is a charity, and having sexual intercourse with your wife is a charity. They (the Companions) said: O Messenger of Allah (ﷺ), is there a reward for him among us who satisfies his sexual passion? He said: Tell me, if he were to devote it to something forbidden, would it not be a sin on his part? Similarly, if he were to devote it to something lawful, he should have a reward.» (Muslim)

Obligations towards one's husband

The most important right of the husband upon the wife is his right to sexual intercourse. The greatest weakness in most women is the desire for economic, physical, and emotional security. Allah (ﷻ) favoured the men in these areas by giving us superior upper body strength as well as sparing us from pregnancy, childbirth, menstruation, postnatal bleeding, menopause, and all the other obstacles He (ﷻ) gave to women. Since Allah gave us the natural ability to maintain, provide, and protect, He (ﷻ) also gave us the responsibility to do so. The greatest weakness in most men, however, is the desire for sexual intercourse with women. The Prophet (ﷺ) stated: «There is no *fitnah* (trial) greater for men than women.» (a sound hadith recorded by at-Tirmidhi)

There are many hadiths about the responsibility of a woman towards her husband when it comes to sexual relations.

The Prophet (ﷺ) said: «When a man invites his wife to bed, she should respond to him, even if she is sitting in a camel's saddle. » (a sound hadith recorded by al-Bazzâr)

The Prophet (ﷺ) said: «When a man invites his wife for his (sexual) need, she should go to him even if she is working at the outdoor oven. » (a sound hadith recorded by an-Nasâ'i and Aḥmad)

The Prophet (ﷺ) said: «If a man invites his wife to bed, and she refuses to come, and he sleeps while angry, the angels curse her until the morning.» (Bukhari and Muslim)

The Prophet (ﷺ) said: «When a woman deserts her husband's bed at night, the angels curse her until the morning.» (Bukhari and Muslim)

The Prophet (ﷺ) said: «By the One in whose hand is my soul, whenever a man invites his wife to his bed and she refuses, the One who is above the heavens will be angry with her until her husband forgives her.» (Muslim)

He (ﷺ) also stated that if a man feels sexually attracted to a woman he sees in the street, he should go home and make love to his wife, because his wife has the same as that woman has. «If one of you is pleased by a woman and something occurs in his heart, he should proceed to his wife and have intercourse with her, as that will repel what is in his soul.» (Muslim)

These hadiths tell us that sexual intercourse should be given freely from one spouse to the other. Sex is not something that should be cheapened until it becomes a commodity that a wife offers or 'sells' to her husband only when he has bought her something or done something else that she wants. When a husband asks his wife to satisfy his sexual desire, then she should freely do so, as long as it will involve no harm to her, since Allah's Messenger (ﷺ) said for all matters: «Harm should neither be inflicted nor reciprocated.» (a sound hadith recorded by Ibn Mâjah) In a similar manner, a husband should do his best to meet the sexual needs of his wife.

A woman should keep herself as physically attractive to her husband as possible. A man should also keep himself well-groomed and smelling nice, so that he does not become offensive to his wife and put her off intimate relations. The Prophet (ﷺ) gave us a great deal of advice in his Sunnah about habits like bathing, cleaning the teeth, trimming the hair of the underarms and pubic region, and using perfume — all of which add to the attraction of one spouse to the other.

A woman must seek her husband's permission to perform voluntary fasts. This is because a person who is fasting must refrain from sexual relations as well as eating and drinking; when the wife is fasting, she will not be available if her husband desires her sexually. Since her main role as a wife is to provide for her husband in that way, she needs his consent.

In Islamic law, the main job of the wife is to provide sexually and emotionally, just as the main job of the husband is to provide economically and physically. This is her main obligation in her marriage, so she must learn how to do it, either through communication or by using instructional books (that do not contain pornography). If she puts forth her maximum effort to please her husband, both sexually and emotionally, then she is considered a great wife.

As regards the average practicing Muslim man, if his wife satisfies him sexually, then inshallah there will be few problems in the marriage from his side. He will be calm, happy and kind to his wife. He will be physically and emotionally relieved and have a big smile on his face. His wife will notice a change in his mannerisms, and he will happily give her more and do more for her.

In contrast, if a husband is not fulfilled sexually, this will lead to many problems in the marriage. In the worst-case scenario, he may be tempted to commit adultery. If he does not do that, he may become involved in some form of unlawful behaviour, such as pornography, cybersex, meeting women in chat rooms, or just going out the house and being flirtatious with other women. If he has too much God-consciousness to do that, then he may reflect his displeasure in his body language towards his wife. He may become dismissive, verbally abusive, passive-aggressive, angry, cranky, or even depressed. It will affect their relationship, as well as his relationship with others such as work colleagues and family members.

Next, a woman is not supposed to let anyone in her house that her husband does not approve of. This is not a license for him to be a tyrant, though, and there are plenty of hadiths that warn men against being tyrants.

Men were given the responsibility to maintain and protect the household and everyone in it. If a man sees that someone who visits his wife is starting trouble in his household, or leading his wife into sin and transgression, then it is his right to tell his wife not to allow this person in the house, and the wife must obey that demand. I know of a case where a man saw that his wife's companion was not good. He realized that the woman would be willing to destroy their marriage to get what she wanted, so he told his wife to stop seeing her. His wife refused to listen to him. Eventually, the woman ended up publicly betraying his wife, who was extremely hurt. She told her husband that if he ever saw anything wrong with someone again, he should tell her, and she would obey him and not entertain that person. She had an emotional connection to the woman, which is why she could not see her poison. The husband did not have that emotional connection and therefore was able to tell his wife the truth about the other woman.

The woman must also protect her husband's wealth and honour. She must not spend his money without his permission, although she is allowed to buy something that is her right but that he is neglecting to provide for her. Narrated 'Â'ishah (ﷺ): «Hind bint 'Utbah (ﷺ) said: O Allah's Apostle, Abu Sufyân is a miser, and he does not give me what is sufficient for me and my children. Can I take of his property without his knowledge? The Prophet (ﷺ) said: Take what is sufficient for you and your children, and the amount should be just and reasonable.» (Bukhari)

Once the Prophet (ﷺ) was asked to judge a case where a child had taken money from his father without permission, because his father was not providing for him although he was giving money to others as charity. The Prophet (ﷺ) ruled in favour of the child; he did not consider his action to be stealing because the boy had a right to that specific provision from his father. However, the boy did not have the right to take beyond what he was owed (and he did not do so).

The wife must not backbite her husband or expose his faults, unless there is a Sharia reason to (such as in court cases, when giving business advice, or when seeking help).

A man needs to feel appreciated by his wife. There are many ways for her to make her husband feel appreciated. She can try to look beautiful for him and make him a good meal when he comes home from work. She can say pleasant things to him and thank him when he does something nice (even if it is something that he is supposed to do). Of course, the same applies to the man as well; when his wife does something nice for him, such as cooking or dressing up for him, he should acknowledge it and thank her.

It can have a serious detrimental effect on the marriage if the wife persistently demonstrates ingratitude. A man may eventually give up on the relationship because he feels like he "can't win". Some women (and men) show ingratitude by belittling any effort and complaining about minor problems, even though the spouse is fulfilling all of the major obligations.

Causes of marital problems and their remedies

There are three general reasons for all marital problems.

1. The husband is not fulfilling his obligations and following the Sunnah, while his wife is.
2. The wife is not fulfilling her obligations and following the Sunnah, while her husband is.
3. Both the husband and wife are neglecting their duties and not following the Sunnah.

If you examine your marriage according to the criteria of the Sunnah, you will probably discover the root causes of all the marital problems you have.

If your husband is not fulfilling his obligations

If your husband is not following the Sunnah and fulfilling your rights, then first try to pull him aside and have a sweet, nice, loving conversation in which you advise him sincerely. At the same time, make supplications frequently, especially at the best of times for supplications.

If he continues to cause problems, go to a male authority figure whom he respects and trusts. Explain the situation to him and ask him to speak to your husband.

If that does not help, try to go to marriage counseling with a trained, certified Muslim counselor.

If that does not work, go to arbitration. If both of you are from righteous Muslim families, have a family member represent each of you in order to try and solve the problem or, if that is not possible, to dissolve the marriage peacefully and amicably. If you are from a non-Muslim family, then get a righteous and fair Muslim to represent you.

If the conflict is still not resolved, then the ruling on divorce depends on what the problem is. There are some issues that would make it obligatory for you to seek a legal release from the marriage. If this matter is affecting your ability to practice your religion and taking you further away from Allah (ﷻ), then it may be considered either a recommended or an obligatory divorce, depending on what the issue is. If it is simply a personality clash, then it can be either a permissible or a detested divorce.

If it is a serious case of physical abuse, go first to the Muslims for help; if that fails, go to the police. Generally speaking, one should not surrender a Muslim to the disbelievers or turn to the disbelievers to resolve a dispute between two Muslims, but there are exceptions to this rule. All human beings have the right to practice their religion, the right to live and be physically safe, and the right to their own wealth and property. If another Muslim is usurping your rights, turn to the Muslims for help. If the Muslims are unable or unwilling to help you and protect your rights, then you may turn to the authorities that can do so, even if they are disbelievers.[42]

If your wife is not fulfilling her obligations

If you are not satisfied in your marriage due to your wife's negligence, monitor your own behaviour and see if there is any sin that you are committing. If there is, you should stop it, repent and see if the problem gets better. If it does, all praise is due to Allah (ﷻ); if not, check to see if you are doing anything to make your wife less attracted to you. Below is a list of things that appeal to women (based on scientific research).

1. A man who treats his wife with true kindness and respect

2. A man whose clothes fit well and are clean and ironed

---

[42] In some cases, you should not wait. For example, if you have certain knowledge that someone you know is about to commit an act of terrorism and affect many lives, you should contact the authorities before their plan comes to fruition. Allowing the person to implement that plan would cause a greater harm than handing over that individual to disbelieving authorities.

3. A man whose hair (and beard) is neat and combed

4. A man who smells good

5. A man whose belt and shoes are not old, worn out, and sloppy looking

6. A man whose teeth are clean and whose breath smells good

7. A man who helps his wife clean the house

8. A man who keeps his car clean

9. A man who is not needy and who has many things going on in his life

10. A man who stands up straight and has good posture

The first item on this list really is 'number one' in terms of importance. This is because a woman's love (and thus sexual attraction) for her husband increases in proportion to the way he fulfils her emotional needs. Her emotional needs are: to know and feel that she is loved and valued for who she is, and to have her husband respect her and not degrade her by calling her names like 'stupid' or 'lazy', or by insulting her family, whether behind closed doors or in front of others.

After studying the Sunnah, I realized that the Prophet (ﷺ) taught men how to be attractive to women. It is no surprise that he (ﷺ) was able to keep so many women happy. The Prophet (ﷺ) was kind and gentle to his wives. He asked their opinions about things, and he did not mock them for what they said or did. He knew when to joke and when to be serious with them. He kept his clothes clean and neat, combed his hair, loved to wear scented oils, cleaned his teeth constantly, and helped his wives with housework. He (ﷺ) was always busy with something and was not needy.

The scientific research shows that women are attracted to men who show them true care and respect, men who take care of themselves independently and who care about themselves. The Prophet (ﷺ) was a self-confident man, one who knew that it did not threaten his position or manhood to show his feelings and his respect for his wives; he (ﷺ) was an independent man who took care of himself and cared about himself. Women feel safe and protected with a self-confident, independent man, and this feeling of security leads them to feel sexually attracted to such men.

If you are doing everything that you are supposed to be doing, and she is still not responding, then talk to her. See if there are physical, mental, or emotional problems; if so, work with her to try to solve those problems. If that is not the case, or if these steps do not work, then take the other measures listed in this section.

If the cause of the conflict is that the wife is not following the Sunnah, then first try to pull her aside and have a sweet, nice, loving conversation in which you advise her sincerely. Make supplications frequently, especially at those times that are best for making supplications.

If that does not work, then you must firmly tell your wife to change her behaviour. If there is no improvement, then you should avoid sleeping in the same bed with her.

If that does not bring about the desired changes, then you should go to arbitration.

A divorce can be obligatory, recommended, permissible, or detested, depending on the situation and its effect on your religion.

If you both are not fulfilling your obligations

If the problem is that both of you are not fulfilling each other's rights and not following the Sunnah, then the two of you must begin to do so.

Another important point is that Islam is fair and just. If one spouse is not fulfilling his or her primary obligations to the other spouse, then the other is not required to fulfil his or her obligations in return.[43]

Polygyny

The Islamic ruling on polygyny [44]

All Muslim scholars agree that it is permissible for a man to have up to four wives as long as he fulfils certain conditions. Scholars of the Shâfi'i school of Islamic law believe that it is recommended for man to only have one wife, and that polygyny is the exception. It is likely that they base this opinion on this verse of the Qur'an:

◖And if you fear that you will not deal justly with the orphan girls, then marry those that please you of [other] women, two or three or four. But if you fear that you will not be just, then [marry only] one or

---

[43] For example, many of the scholars of Islam state in the books of fiqh that if a woman is not fulfilling her obligations to her spouse, then the husband does not have to provide her with shelter and clothing, or fulfil her other rights, because she is not fulfilling his rights, and vice versa. See al-Fawzan, *A Summary of Islamic Jurisprudence Volume 2*.

[44] Many Western nonbelievers, and the Muslims who are following them down the lizard hole, have a problem with polygyny. Many of them are ethnocentric people who want every culture in the world to follow them; the Qur'an states that these people will not be satisfied until we follow them in everything. The fact is that males are naturally inclined to be polygamous, and this creates problems in Western society, which has not found a way to address this problem without causing more problems in the end. Islam is not a legal code that was created by specific people for specific times and places. It is a flexible, moral and legal code that can be adapted to every culture in the world. Islam did not come to force the world's polygamous cultures (estimated to be eighty-four percent of them) into monogamy. Rather, it came to solve the problems of every culture in the world; as such, it can be applied equally throughout the world in every time, in every place, and in every culture.

those your right hands possess. That is more suitable that you may not incline [to injustice].❫   *(Qur'an 4: 3)*

Other scholars state that it is recommended for a man to have more than one wife.

After examining the two positions within the overall objectives of the Sharia, it appears to me that neither is totally correct. Celibacy and monasticism are against the religion of Islam. Islam teaches that every man should have a wife, and every woman should have a husband.

Now, if every man in the world had four wives, there would be plenty of unmarried men. This would lead to many social problems in the world including wars, murder, homosexuality, rape, child molestation and the like. Therefore, this cannot be applied globally. On the other hand, if every man had only one wife, there would be millions and millions of women with no husbands, and this would cause many other social problems.

Therefore, the ruling of polygyny should be practiced within the context of particular cultures. The purpose of polygyny is to make sure that every woman can have a husband and be emotionally satisfied. In a society where the ratio of men to women is close to being equal, monogamy would be the norm, and polygyny would be the exception. In a society where there are far more women than men, polygyny would be the norm.

For whom is polygyny permissible, and how does it work?

Polygyny is permissible for any man who can fulfil all of the rights of more than one woman, including providing for them financially. The man has to treat his wives justly, and he must divide his time equally among them. Each wife has a right to her own housing accommodations, food, clothing and products she needs to beautify herself. Each wife must be provided for according to her needs and according to the customary level in that society (into which she has married), which may or may not be the level that her father had provided for her. If a husband buys a dress for one wife, he must buy one for his other wives as well. When it comes to housing, a wife with more children can have a bigger house than a wife with fewer children because the children need more rooms as well.

A husband cannot make the wives live together in the same housing unit unless they agree. Even then, if a wife asks for separate accommodations at any time, he must provide it, because it is her right.

In modern times, women often work and pay their own expenses. It is permissible for a woman to relinquish her rights to financial maintenance and enter into polygyny if there is a need in the community. For example, there might be many women, but a shortage of men who are able to provide for two wives — thus leading to many women being unmarried.

Divorce

Many 'cultural' Muslims will hate reading this section because so much innovation has crept into their minds when it comes to marriage. Many Muslims have imitated the Hindus and the Christians by embracing their creeds regarding marriage.

Many so-called Muslims see marriage as a permanent agreement that should never end, as well as a permanent joining of two families. They see divorce as something evil, and they stigmatize divorced Muslims and pass judgment on them — especially on the Muslim sisters. Using many weak and fabricated hadiths, which actually contradict the Sunnah, they try to scare Muslims away from divorce even when they are suffering in mentally, physically, and verbally abusive marriages. They quote fabricated hadiths such as

"The most hateful of all permissible things to Allah is divorce,"[45] and even then they sometimes omit the word 'permissible' when quoting that fake hadith, because it does not suit their desires.

When I was sitting down to go through my divorce, an imam quoted a disgusting, fabricated hadith in order to scare us into not getting divorced. He claimed that the Prophet (ﷺ) said that the angels curse the woman who gets divorced, and that they keep praying for Allah (ﷻ) to curse her (or something similar to that). The Prophet (ﷺ) never said such a thing, and this contradicts the word of Allah (ﷻ), who gave the women the right to be released from the marriage (in exchange for a payment, usually involving the return of her bridal gift). It also contradicts the practice of the Companions (may Allah be pleased with them), many of whom got divorced.

In an authentic hadith, the Prophet (ﷺ) said: «Stick to my Sunnah and the sunnah of the Rightly-guided Caliphs.» (a sound hadith recorded by Aḥmad, al-Hâkim and Ibn Mâjah)

If we examine their way, we find that 'Umar (ﷺ), for example, got divorced four times — twice before Islam and twice as a Muslim.[46] The fifth caliph, Ḥasan (ﷺ), the grandson of the Prophet (ﷺ), was divorced dozens of times. The Prophet (ﷺ) was going to divorce one of his wives (may Allah be pleased with them), but she promised to give up the days when the Prophet (ﷺ) would sleep at her house, and give them to 'Â'ishah (ﷺ) instead, so he (ﷺ) agreed to stay married to her. The Companions of the Prophet (may

---

[45] Shaykh al-Albâni and other scholars have spoken and written extensively about these issues and how these fabricated hadiths are affecting the Muslim Ummah. Aboo Tasneem Dâwood Adeeb, an American caller to Islam, has covered this as well in his lectures, such as "Using Weak and Fabricated Ahadith".

[46] The two wives he divorced as a Muslim were Maleekah bint Jarwal and Quraybah bint Abi Umayyah al-Makhzoomi.

Allah be pleased with them) had a very high divorce rate, and many of them married divorced women; they did not judge the woman or the man, or view them as immoral, simply because they had been divorced. They realized that people sometimes got divorced because their personalities were no longer compatible and the marriage was not working out.

This was the way of the Companions (may Allah be pleased with them) and the Sunnah of the Rightly-guided Caliphs (may Allah be pleased with them). If the marriage works, the couple should stay together; if not, they should try to resolve the problems, but if they are unable to do so, then they can marry other people. When it comes to marriage, we need to return to the understanding of the first three generations of Muslims and destroy the filthy, disgusting innovations that Muslims brought into the religion by their imitation of the Christians and the Hindus. Remember the following hadiths:

«You will indeed follow the ways of those who came before you, hand-span by hand-span and arms-length by arms-length, to the extent that if they were to enter a lizard's hole, then you would likewise follow them. We said: O Messenger of Allah! Do you mean the Jews and Christians? He said: Who else?» (Bukhari and Muslim)

«Every innovation is an error that leads astray, and every error that leads astray is in the hellfire.» (a sound hadith recorded by Ibn Mâjah)

Actually, the Sharia ruling on divorce depends on the situation. It can fall under the category of obligatory, recommended, permissible, detested, or forbidden, according to the circumstances.

It should be clear from the examples above that divorce is allowable and was the practice of many of the Companions (may Allah be pleased with them). This knowledge should inshallah help to change the negative attitudes that people in many Muslim communities have about divorce and about divorced people. However, the fact remains that divorce often exposes Muslim women to extreme vulnerability, both financially and socially. Statistically speaking, a divorced woman with children is at a higher risk of falling into poverty.[47] In the Muslim populations in the U.S. and elsewhere, this risk is increased, since many Muslim women marry young, stay home to bear and raise children, and never enter the job market. If they are divorced, these woman may find themselves with no source of financial support for themselves or their children.

Consider the case of a woman in her early forties who has always been a stay-at-home mom. She suddenly finds herself divorced, with her husband remarried. If the ex-husband does not willingly provide her with support, then she either has to seek it through the court system (which is expensive and exhausting) or try to earn money herself just to survive and feed her children. Her parents may be non-Muslims who do not feel obligated to bring her back into their home and support her. Even if they happen to be Muslims who know that they are once again obligated to provide for her, by this time the woman's father has most likely already retired and the family is living on a fixed income, unable to support the divorced daughter and her children.

In countries whose laws are supposedly based on Islamic Sharia, the situation is often worse. If the woman has custody of her children, it often happens that the children's father 'forgets' about his children, especially once he remarries (which is usually pretty quickly). The divorced woman has to decide whether to seek her rights through the courts (expensive, difficult, and likely to make the neighbours and relatives speak badly of her) or to try to find any

---

[47] Wood, "Effect of child and family poverty on child health in the United States", 2003

menial job just to try to feed and clothe her children. If the woman is not granted custody of her children, she has the agony of being separated from them, and unless the ex-husband is sensitive to the needs of his children and his ex-wife, the mother may go months or even years without being allowed to see her children. In many 'Muslim' countries, divorced women may be ostracized by their families or even forced into a position of servitude. It is not uncommon to find a divorced woman living in the home of her married brother. (As her maḥram, he is obliged to take care of her if she has no husband and her father is either dead or unable to provide for her). It is very easy for the divorced woman's weak position to be taken advantage of; I have heard of cases where the woman's own brother turns away any and all suitors for her hand in marriage, just so that he can keep her as an unpaid worker in his home. Due to her vulnerable position and lack of legal options, she can do nothing about it.

So while it is important to know that divorce should be seen as more acceptable in the Muslim community, it is also important to realize the great gap between what divorce means in real terms in a man's life and what it means in a woman's life. I want to caution my brother Muslims to act carefully and to fear Allah (ﷻ) when dealing with their ex-wives and their children from them.

Lastly, always perform the prayer for guidance[48] before making major decisions such as marriage, divorce, and job change.

---

[48] This prayer is described in the chapter 'Seeking Help with Life's Decisions'.

Parent-Child Conflict: Causes and Solutions

$\mathcal{M}$any Western Muslims are facing challenges, and these challenges are causing conflicts between parents and children. Often, parents refer to specific Qur'anic verses and hadiths to use religion as a means of oppression. In reality, Islam provides balance and justice. After reading this chapter, parents will know the rights and responsibilities that Islam gives them, and children will know the rights and responsibilities that Islam gives them. Inshallah both will be able to determine who is at fault when there is a conflict between a parent and a child, and they will know how to resolve it.

Rights of parents

The parents have certain rights in Islam.[49] Their children should speak lovingly and respectfully to them. Children must obey their parents in all matters, with a few exceptions. The following verses and hadiths stress the rights of parents.

◄And We have enjoined upon man [care] for his parents. His mother carried him, [increasing her] in weakness upon weakness, and his weaning is in two years. Be grateful to Me and to your parents; to Me is the [final] destination. But if they endeavor to make you associate with Me that of which you have no knowledge, do not obey them but accompany them in [this] world with appropriate kindness and follow the way of those who turn back to Me [in repentance]. Then to Me will be your return, and I will inform you about what you used to do.► *(Qur'an 31: 14-15)*

---

[49] Generally speaking, your spouse's parents have rights similar to your parents, but a degree lower.

❨And We have enjoined upon man, to his parents, good treatment. His mother carried him with hardship and gave birth to him with hardship, and his gestation and weaning [period] is thirty months...❩

(Qur'an 46: 15)

❨And your Lord has decreed that you not worship except Him, and to parents, good treatment. Whether one or both of them reach old age [while] with you, say not to them [so much as] 'uff ', and do not repel them but speak to them a noble word. And lower to them the wing of humility out of mercy and say: My Lord, have mercy upon them as they brought me up [when I was] small.❩   *(Qur'an 17: 23-24)*

«Once a man came to the Prophet (ﷺ) and asked: Who is most deserving of my good companionship? The Prophet (ﷺ) replied: Your mother. The man asked: Who next? The Prophet (ﷺ) replied: Your mother. The man asked: Who next? The Prophet (ﷺ) replied: Your mother. The man asked: Who next? The Prophet (ﷺ) replied: Your father.» (Bukhari and Muslim)

«The Prophet (ﷺ) said: Shall I not inform you about the three major sins? Those who were present replied: Yes, O Messenger of Allah. He said: Associating partners with Allah and disobedience to parents. Sitting up from the reclining position, he continued: and telling lies and false testimony; beware of them.» (Bukhari and Muslim)

«'Abdullah ibn 'Amr ibn al-'Âṣ (﵂) narrated: A man came to the Prophet (ﷺ) and said: I give the oath of allegiance to you to emigrate (to Madinah) and serve in combat, seeking reward from Allah (ﷻ). The Prophet (ﷺ) asked whether either of his parents was living. When he replied that both of them were, the Prophet (ﷺ) said: Are you (really) seeking reward from Allah? The man said yes. The Prophet (ﷺ) then said: Go back to your parents and be a good companion to them.» (Muslim)

«'Abdullah ibn 'Amr ibn al-'Âṣ (ﷺ) narrated that a man came to the Prophet (ﷺ) and said: I have come to swear allegiance to you to migrate (to Madinah), and I have left my parents weeping. The Prophet (ﷺ) said to him: Return to them and make them laugh as you made them weep.» (Bukhari)

Even though his migration was an obligation, this man still had to comfort his parents when fulfilling this obligation. For those of us who are converts to Islam, we must keep this in mind when dealing with our non-Muslim relatives. If we hurt the feelings of our parents by telling them that we can no longer do something because it is prohibited by the Sharia, we should go back and comfort them by doing something with them that is permissible. However, we do not compromise in our religion, because the Prophet (ﷺ) said: «There is no obedience to the creation in disobedience to the Creator.» (a sound hadith recorded by Aḥmad and al-Hâkim)

When can one disobey one's parents?

There are certain occasions when you can disobey your parents. For example:

1. When they tell you to do something that goes against the Sharia.

2. When they try to force you to marry someone whom you do not want to marry. «'Â'ishah (ﷺ) narrates that the Prophet (ﷺ) said: A virgin's consent must be sought for marriage. To this 'Â'ishah commented: But a virgin is too bashful. The Prophet (ﷺ) replied: Her silence is her consent.» (Bukhari)

3. When they try to force you into a certain career path. Individuals have the right to be happy, as long as that does not mean disobeying Allah (ﷻ). When you leave your parents' house, much of your time will be spent with your spouse or on your career. If you are miserable doing what you do, this will cause great harm in your life and in society. Most of the time today,

parents who try to force their children to choose a certain career, or to marry certain people, do not do so for the sake of Allah (ﷻ); they are simply trying to boost their egos. They want to brag to their friends and family that their child is a doctor who married another doctor. They do not care whether this marriage will make the child happy in life or whether the child will enjoy life as a doctor. Many times, they do not even care about the safety of their children's religion. All they care about is the satisfaction of their own ego, for which they will sacrifice their children. These disgusting, filthy innovations need to stop.

Shaykh Siddiqui dealt with this issue when a question was posed to him on Pakistanlink.

"Question: I want to become a journalist, but my parents say that I have to be a doctor when I grow up. Why can't I just make my own decisions?

Answer: Parents' responsibility is to see that whatever their children do is permissible in Islam and they do it with serious commitment. According to Islam, you have every right to choose your own career. You should do what you feel you can do best. Journalism is a very important profession, and it is very much needed. We need very good Muslim journalists who can present Islamic viewpoints in a professional manner. Talk to your parents nicely and try to convince them that you can do well as a journalist also. If they need to discuss this matter further, take them to some counselors who can help them understand that journalism could also be a good and successful profession. I wish you all the best."

Note, however, that if your parents are paying for your college education, they have a right to tell you what to study. If you want to study something else and they refuse, then you have to start paying for your own education.

4. When they try to force you to divorce your spouse.

5. When obeying them could be destructive to your marriage or your life. The Prophet (ﷺ) said: «Harm should neither be inflicted nor reciprocated.» (a sound hadith recorded by Ibn Mâjah) He (ﷺ) also said: «There is no obedience to the creation in disobedience to the Creator.» (a sound hadith recorded by Aḥmad and al-Hâkim) Since doing something harmful to yourself or others is disobeying Allah (ﷻ), you cannot obey your parents in this instance.

Rights of children

According to Islam, the parents are supposed to provide their children with love, affection, discipline, food, shelter and clothes. They should spend time with them, play with them, and help them to acquire and implement knowledge of the Qur'an, Sunnah, Sharia, and purification of the heart from spiritual diseases (which is the main subject of this book). Their job is not to force their children into a certain career, to force them to marry someone of a particular tribe or nationality, to neglect them, to give them a Play Station (video game console) and tell them to go play with it and leave their parents alone, to fail to provide for them, to neglect to teach them the religion, or to try to override the teachings of Islam with the innovations of their culture.

To reiterate, children have a right to:

1. food, water, shelter and clothing
2. love and affection[50]

---

[50] «'Â'ishah (ؓ) said: A desert Arab came to the Messenger of Allah (ﷺ) and said: Do you kiss children? We do not kiss them. The Messenger of Allah said: What can I do for you if Allah has taken away mercy from your heart?» (Bukhari and Muslim)=

3. discipline[51]

4. to be taught the principles of tawḥeed, the Sharia (which covers the rules concerning acts of worship; major sins; what is permissible and what is prohibited in daily life, marriage, choice of careers, and any other matters in which they will be involved, according to the Qur'an and authentic Sunnah), proper pronunciation and recitation of the Qur'an, and purification of the heart.

5. to be treated equally and not to be shown favouritism[52]

Children are under our care, but they are not our slaves. We guide them, but we do not tyrannize or oppress them.

=From 'Amr ibn Shu'ayb, from his father, from his grandfather: «The Messenger of Allah (ﷺ) said: He is not of us who has no compassion for our little ones and does not honour our old ones.» (a sound hadith recorded by Abu Dâwood and at-Tirmidhi)

[51] From 'Amr ibn Shu'ayb, from his father, from his grandfather, who said: The Messenger of Allah (ﷺ) said: «Prescribe prayers to your children when they are seven years of age, and punish them (if they do not say them) when they are ten years of age, and separate their beds (at that age).» (a reliable hadith recorded by Abu Dâwood)

[52] Nu'mân ibn Basheer (﵁) narrated: «My father presented a gift to me, and my mother asked him to go to the Messenger of Allah (ﷺ) and ask him to be a witness to that. My father went to the Messenger of Allah and said to him: I presented my son Nu'mân with a gift, and (his mother) 'Amrah asked me to make you a witness to that. The Prophet (ﷺ) asked Basheer: Do you have other sons besides him? Basheer said yes. The Prophet said: And you gave all of them the like of what you gave Nu'mân? Basheer said no. The Prophet (ﷺ) said: This is an injustice. Look for another person to be a witness to it! He then added: Don't you want all of your children to be dutiful to you? Basheer said yes. The Prophet then said: As you have a right that they should all be equally dutiful to and compassionate with you, they also have a right to receive equal treatment from you.» (a sound hadith recorded by Abu Dâwood)
«The Prophet (ﷺ) said: Fear Allah and treat your children with equal justice.» (Bukhari and Muslim)

Why are my children rebellious?

The vast majority of the time, if your children are rebellious, it is because you are not fully following the Sunnah and the Sharia in your parenting. Children and teenagers are not naturally rebellious; it is something that they have been taught through television shows in the West. The vast majority of children will behave correctly if you are following the Sunnah and the Sharia completely. If you are like the Prophet (ﷺ), your children will be like Anas ibn Mâlik (رضي الله عنه) and 'Abdullah ibn 'Abbâs (رضي الله عنه).

Who causes the fitnah?

When things in your life are not going the way that you want, it is your fault the vast majority of the time. If your relationship is not going well with your spouse, children, parents, family members, or in any other areas in your life, weigh your behaviour and actions against the Sunnah. Are you acting the way the Prophet Muhammad (ﷺ) would have acted? Most of the time, your problems occur because your lower self, or ego, is in opposition to the Sunnah. The Sunnah is your path to internal happiness; it leads to contentment, which is true wealth.

Stop blaming others and start blaming yourself. If your children are not following the Sharia in one area of their life, it is most likely because you are not following the Sharia in another area. Weigh yourself against the Sharia and try to figure it out. When you establish your actions according to the Sunnah and the Sharia, you may find it difficult at first, but this will be followed by long-term ease. When you act against the Sunnah and the Sharia, you will avoid the initial discomfort, but you will endure a lifetime of difficulties, hurt and discomfort.

This is a message for parents whose children have fully embraced Islam or who are trying to receive their Islamic rights: The imam, speaker or writer who teaches your children the Sunnah and the correct understanding of Islamic law is not causing fitnah when your children start following the whole Sunnah and the whole Sharia. On the contrary, you are causing the fitnah by not following the Sunnah and the Sharia in their entirety. You are causing the fitnah by making your culture a legislative partner with Allah (ﷻ) and by trying to force upon your children laws other than the laws of Allah (ﷻ). Remember this.

Preventing Problems
with Neighbours

$\mathcal{T}$he Prophet (ﷺ) taught us how to treat our neighbours. If we followed his advice, we would have few — if any — problems in our neighbourhoods.

Your neighbour must be safe

«Abu Hurayrah (رضي الله عنه) narrated that the Messenger of Allah (ﷺ) said: By Allah, he does not (truly) believe! By Allah, he does not (truly) believe! By Allah, he does not (truly) believe! Someone asked: Who, O Messenger of Allah? He (ﷺ) said: He whose neighbour is not safe from his mischief.» (Bukhari and Muslim)

'Â'ishah (رضي الله عنها) reported that the Prophet (ﷺ) said: «*Jibreel* — the angel Gabriel — (عليه السلام) kept on recommending that I treat neighbours well, until I thought that he would order me to treat them as my heirs.» (Bukhari)

Abu Shurayh al-Khuzâ'i (رضي الله عنه) reported that the Prophet (ﷺ) said: «Anyone who believes in Allah (ﷻ) and the Last Day should be good to his neighbours. Anyone who believes in Allah and the Last Day should be generous to his guest. Anyone who believes in Allah and the Last Day should be say what is good or be silent.» (Bukhari)

Ibn 'Umar (رضي الله عنه) said: «There was a time when no one was more entitled to a person's money than his Muslim brother. Now people love their *dirham*s (silver coins) and *dinar*s (gold coins) more than their Muslim brother. I heard the Prophet (ﷺ) say: How many a neighbour will be brought together with his neighbour on the Day of

Rising! He will say: Lord, this man closed his door to me and refused to show me common kindness.» (Bukhari)

'Abdullah ibn 'Amr ibn al-'Âs (ﷺ) reported that the Messenger of Allah (ﷺ) said: «The best of companions in the sight of Allah (ﷺ) is the best of them towards his companion, and the best of neighbours in the sight of Allah is the best of them towards his neighbour.» (Bukhari)

Abu Hurayrah (ﷺ) reported that the Messenger of Allah (ﷺ) said: «A person whose neighbours are not safe from his evil will not enter paradise. (Bukhari)

Share your food with your neighbours and give them gifts

«Mujâhid reported that a sheep was slaughtered for 'Abdullah ibn 'Amr. He asked his servant: Have you given any to our Jewish neighbour? Have you given any to our Jewish neighbour? I heard the Messenger of Allah (ﷺ) say: Jibreel (ﷺ) kept on recommending that I treat my neighbours well, until I thought that he would order me to treat them as my heirs.» (Bukhari's *Al-Adab wal Mufrad*)

«'Â'ishah (ﷺ) said: I said: Messenger of Allah (ﷺ), I have two neighbours. To whom should I give my gifts? He replied: To the one whose door is nearer to you.» (Bukhari)

Al-Ḥasan (ﷺ) was asked about the neighbour, and he said, "The term 'neighbour' includes the forty houses in front a person, the forty houses behind him, the forty houses on his right and the forty houses on his left." (Bukhari)

Ibn 'Abbâs (ﷺ) told Ibn az-Zubayr (ﷺ) that he heard the Prophet (ﷺ) say: «A man is not a believer who fills his stomach while his neighbour is hungry.» (Bukhari)

«It is reported that Abu Dharr (ؓ) said: My dear friend [the Prophet (ﷺ)] enjoined three things on me: Hear and obey, even if the ruler is a slave with his limbs amputated. When you cook a stew, put a lot of water in it and then go and see the people of a neighbouring house and give them a reasonable amount of it. Pray the prayers at their proper times, then if you find that the imam has already prayed, you have guarded your prayer (by already having performed it). If not, it is a supererogatory prayer (since you have done it again).» (Bukhari)

Preventing Problems with Other Muslims

*B*oth the Qur'an and Sunnah teach us that all Muslims are brothers and sisters and are part of one body. Just like families related by blood, spiritual families have conflicts as well. We cannot solve all the conflicts of the Ummah; however, we can do our part to stop the fitnah instead of doing our part to spread the fitnah. We do our part in solving the problems of the Ummah by knowing the rights of other Muslims and giving them those rights.

Rights of the Muslims

'Abdullah ibn 'Umar (ﷺ) narrated that the Messenger of Allah (ﷺ) said: «The Muslim is he from whose tongue and hand a Muslim is safe, and the emigrant is he who gives up what Allah (ﷺ) has prohibited for him.» (Bukhari and Muslim)

Abu Hurayrah (ﷺ) reported that the Messenger of Allah (ﷺ) said: «Every Muslim has five rights over another Muslim: to return the greetings, to visit the sick, to accompany funeral processions, to accept an invitation, to respond to the sneezer.» (Bukhari and Muslim)

A Muslim greets another Muslim with *assalâmu 'alaykum* (peace be upon you), and the second Muslim returns the greeting by saying *wa 'alaykum assalâm* (and upon you peace). When one sneezes, he or she says *alhamdulillâh* (all praise is for Allah); another Muslim responds by saying *yarhamkum Allah* (may Allah have mercy on you).

«Abu Hurayrah (ﷺ) reported that the Messenger of Allah (ﷺ) said: Beware of suspicion, for suspicion is the greatest falsehood. Do not try to find fault with each other, do not spy on one another, do not vie with one another, do not envy one another, do not be angry with one another, do not turn away from one another, and be servants of Allah (ﷻ), brothers to one another.» (Bukhari and Muslim)

The Prophet (ﷺ) also said: «A Muslim is the brother of a Muslim. He does him no wrong, nor does he let him down, nor does he despise him. Fear of Allah (ﷻ) is here, fear of Allah is here (and he pointed to his chest). It is evil enough that a Muslim should look down on his brother. For every Muslim is sacred to one another: his blood, his honour and his property. Allah (ﷻ) does not look at your bodies or your forms or your deeds, but He looks at your hearts.» (Muslim)

Ibn 'Umar (ﺭ) narrated that the Messenger of Allah (ﷺ) said: «O you who declare Islam with your tongues but whose hearts have not been reached by faith, do not annoy the Muslims nor seek out their faults, for he who seeks out the faults of his brother Muslim will have his faults sought out by Allah (ﷻ), and when Allah seeks out someone's faults, He exposes them, even if he is in the interior of his house.» (Bukhari and Muslim)

Abu Ayyoob al-Anṣâri (ﺭ) reported that the Messenger of Allah (ﷺ) said: «It is not right for a man to abandon his brother for more than three days.» (Bukhari and Muslim)

Preventing Problems
with Non-Muslims

$\mathcal{T}$here is so much confusion today — amongst Muslims and non-Muslims alike — about how Muslims should treat non-Muslims. There are many reasons for this confusion. One major reason is that people read the Qur'an and hadiths without proper background knowledge of the legal and contextual implications of the texts themselves.

The Qur'an was revealed gradually over a period of twenty-three years, and the Sunnah includes the sayings and actions of the Prophet (ﷺ) throughout those same years. During this time, there were periods of peace, persecution, and war, so different Qur'anic verses and hadiths came as a result of diverse situations. Muslims are supposed to be kind to non-Muslims who are not at war with us or persecuting us. However, when Muslims are being persecuted or engaged in warfare, we are to be harsh and stern, in order to put fear in the enemy and make sure they will not want to repeat this behaviour. A Muslim should be like the boy on the playground who is normally friendly, nice and fair to everyone. However, when a bully tries to intimidate him or others, he beats the bully so badly that the bully — and everyone else — will think twice about threatening him again. Once the boy is respected, and he knows that people are not going to try and harm him, he can go back to being nice.

Many of the enemies of Islam, both from within (such as the Kharijites, who will be discussed more in the section on terrorism) and from the non-Muslims, take passages from the Qur'an and hadiths, as well as statements from some Muslim scholars of the past (usually those who wrote their books during periods of war), and try to interpret them to justify ill treatment towards non-Muslims. In truth, though, the Muslims should be balanced. The Qur'an and Sunnah teach us to be nice, kind, and charitable in general. At the same time, Islam teaches us to have dignity and to not let people think that we are weak and can be treated with disrespect. Below, I have listed some texts that teach us how non-Muslims should be treated.

Kindness towards humanity in general

❨Allah does not forbid you from those who do not fight you because of religion and do not expel you from your homes — from being righteous toward them and acting justly toward them. Indeed, Allah loves those who act justly. Allah only forbids you from those who fight you because of religion and expel you from your homes and aid in your expulsion — [forbids] that you make allies of them. And whoever makes allies of them, then it is those who are the wrongdoers.❩   *(Qur'an 60: 8-9)*

Strength and toughness towards those who fight against and persecute Muslims

❨...Allah will bring forth [in place of them] a people He will love and who will love Him [who are] humble toward the believers, powerful against the disbelievers...❩   *(Qur'an 5: 54)*

The previous verse is in reference to how Muslims should be on the battlefield in a war where they have been mocked, attacked, and persecuted by non-Muslims.

❨And it has already come down to you in the Book that when you hear the verses of Allah [recited], they are denied [by them] and ridiculed; so do not sit with them until they enter into another conversation. Indeed, you would then be like them. Indeed Allah will gather the hypocrites and disbelievers in hell all together.》

(Qur'an 4: 140)

Protecting non-Muslims under the care of Muslims

Non-Muslim residents of Islamic nations, who are protected or covenanted, are called *dhimmis*. The Prophet (ﷺ) said: «If anyone oppresses a dhimmi or burdens him with something he cannot bear, I will argue against him on the Day of Judgment.» (a sound hadith recorded by Abu Dâwood and Bayhaqi)

Not insulting the religions of other people

《And do not insult those they invoke other than Allah, lest they insult Allah in enmity without knowledge. Thus We have made pleasing to every community their deeds. Then to their Lord is their return, and He will inform them about what they used to do.》 *(Qur'an 6: 108)*

Wanting good for them

The Prophet (ﷺ) said: «None of you truly believes until he loves for (all) human beings what he loves for himself.» (Bukhari)

Sanctity of human life

The Prophet (ﷺ) said: «Whoever kills a person with whom we have a treaty will not come close enough to paradise to smell its scent, and its scent can be found as far away as forty years of travel.» (Bukhari)

Solving Problems by
Practicing the Sunnah Daily

$\mathcal{P}$racticing the Sunnah is the key to a happy life. The more of the Sunnah you implement in your life, the happier you will be. The Qur'an states:

❨There has certainly been for you in the Messenger of Allah an excellent pattern for anyone whose hope is in Allah and the Last Day and [who] remembers Allah often.❩ *(Qur'an 33: 21)*

When studying the life of the Prophet (ﷺ), we can see balance. He (ﷺ) gave appropriate amounts of time to Allah (ﷻ), his wives and family (may Allah be pleased with them), his job, his community and his own physical needs. He (ﷺ) did not go to extremes in any of these areas; nor did he neglect any of them.

In this section, we will go through a day with the Prophet Muhammad (ﷺ) and learn how he lived on a regular basis. We should try to implement as much of this information as we are able. However, we must realize that Muslims living in predominantly non-Muslim communities most likely cannot implement the Sunnah completely. If that is the case with you, then do as much as you are able and continually strive to do more. The hadiths and verse below should be encouragement to those Muslims who cannot do as much as they would like to.

«Narrated Ṭalḥah ibn 'Ubaydullah (ﷺ): A man came to Allah's Apostle (ﷺ) asking him about Islam. Allah's Apostle (ﷺ) said: You have to offer five compulsory prayers in a day and a night (a twenty-four hour period). The man asked: Is there any more compulsory prayer for me? Allah's Apostle (ﷺ) said: No, unless you would like to offer optional prayers. Allah's Apostle (ﷺ) then added:

You have to observe fasts during the month of Ramadan. The man said: Am I to fast any other days? Allah's Apostle (ﷺ) said: No, unless you wish to observe the optional fast voluntarily. Then Allah's Apostle (ﷺ) told him about the compulsory zakâh. The man asked: Do I have to give anything besides? Allah's Apostle (ﷺ) said: No, unless you wish to give in charity voluntarily. So the man departed, saying: By Allah, I will neither do more nor less than that. Allah's Apostle (ﷺ) said: If he has said the truth, he will be successful.» (Bukhari and Muslim)

«Abu 'Abdullah Jâbir ibn 'Abdullah al-Anṣâri (رضي الله عنه) reported that a man questioned the Messenger of Allah (ﷺ), saying: Shall I enter paradise if I pray the prescribed (prayers), fast during Ramadan, treat the lawful as permissible and treat the forbidden as prohibited, but do nothing more than that? He (ﷺ) answered: Yes. The man added: I will do nothing more.» (Muslim)

Abu Hurayrah (رضي الله عنه) narrated that the Prophet (ﷺ) stated: «Allah (ﷻ) said: I will declare war against him who shows hostility to a pious worshipper of Mine. The most beloved things with which My slave comes nearer to Me are what I have enjoined upon him, and My slave keeps on coming closer to Me through performing extra deeds (besides what is obligatory) until I love him. I become his sense of hearing with which he hears, his sense of sight with which he sees, his hand with which he grips, and his leg with which he walks. If he asks Me, I will give him, and if he asks My protection, I will protect him. I do not hesitate to do anything as I hesitate to take the soul of the believer, for he hates death, and I hate to disappoint him.» (Bukhari)

❝So fear Allah as much as you are able and listen and obey and spend [in the way of Allah]; it is better for your selves. And whoever is protected from the stinginess of his soul — it is those who will be the successful.❞ *(Qur'an 64: 16)*

Abu Hurayrah (ﷺ) narrated that the Prophet (ﷺ) said: «Religion is very easy, and whoever overburdens himself in his religion will not be able to continue in that way. So you should not be extremists, but try to be near to perfection and receive the good tidings that you will be rewarded; gain strength by worshipping in the mornings and the nights.» (Bukhari and an-Nasâ'i)

When waking up

الْحَمْدُ لِلَّهِ الَّذِي أَحْيَانَا بَعْدَ مَا أَمَاتَنَا وَإِلَيْهِ النُّشُورُ

You should say, *"Alḥamdu lillâhil-ladhee aḥyânâ ba'da mâ amâtanâ wa ilayhin-nushoor.* [All praise is for Allah who gave us life after having taken it from us, and unto Him is the resurrection.]"[53]

الْحَمْدُ لِلَّهِ الَّذِي عَافَانِي فِي جَسَدِي، وَرَدَّ عَلَيَّ رُوحِي، وَأَذِنَ لِي بِذِكْرِهِ

Then say, *"Alḥamdu lillâhil-ladhee 'âfânee fee jasadee, wa radda 'alayya rooḥee, wa adhina lee bithikrih.* [All praise is for Allah who restored to me my health and returned my soul and has allowed me to remember Him.]"

Afterwards recite verses (3: 190-200) of the Qur'an.[54]

Before going to the bathroom

[بِسْمِ اللَّهِ] اللَّهُمَّ إِنِّي أَعُوذُ بِكَ مِنَ الْخُبْثِ وَالْخَبَائِثِ

(Before entering) Say, *"Bismillâh.* [In the name of Allah.]" (Then) *"Allâhumma innee a'oodhu bika min al-khubuthi walkhabâ'ith.* [O Allah! I seek refuge in You from evil, and from all malicious beings.]" Then enter with your left foot first.

---

[53] The English translations of many of the supplications in this section have been adapted from those found at www.makedua.com

[54] Sabiq, *Fiqh us-Sunnah*, Vol. 2, 22

Choose the secluded stall (not the open urinals), and wash your private parts with water after you finish urinating

Anas ibn Mâlik (رضي الله عنه) said: «The Messenger (ﷺ) used to seclude himself, and I and a boy like me used to carry some water for him and his spear, and he washed himself with water.» (Bukhari and Muslim)

Clean your private parts using your left hand

Abu Qatâdah al-Ḥârith ibn Rabee' (رضي الله عنه) reported that the Prophet (ﷺ) said: «None of you should hold his private part with his right hand while he is urinating, and he should not clean himself from stool and urine with his right hand.» (Bukhari and Muslim)

Do not converse while urinating

«Ibn 'Umar (رضي الله عنه) related that a man passed by the Prophet (ﷺ) and greeted him while he (the Prophet) was urinating. The Prophet (ﷺ) did not return his greeting.» (Muslim)

When leaving the bathroom

غُفْرَانَكَ

Exit with your right foot first and say, "*Ghufrânak*. [I ask You (Allah) for forgiveness.]"

When getting dressed

الْحَمْدُ لِلَّهِ الَّذِي كَسَانِي هَذَا (الثَّوبَ) وَرَزَقَنِيهِ مِنْ غَيْرِ حَوْلٍ مِنِّي وَلاَ قُوَّةٍ

Say, "*Alḥamdu lillâhil-ladhee kasânee hâdhâ (ath-thawb) wa razaqaneehi min ghayri ḥawlin minnee wa lâ quwwah.* [All praise is for Allah, Who has clothed me with this garment and provided it for me, with no power or might from myself.]" (Bukhari, Muslim, Abu Dâwood, at-Tirmidhi and Ibn Mâjah)

After using the bathroom, the Prophet (ﷺ) would make ablution and then perform two short units of prayer before heading to the mosque.

When leaving the home

بِسْمِ اللَّهِ، تَوَكَّلْتُ عَلَى اللَّهِ، وَلاَ حَوْلَ وَلاَ قُوَّةَ إِلاَّ بِاللَّهِ

Say, "*Bismillâhi, tawakkaltu 'alallâhi, wa lâ ḥawla wa lâ quwwata illâ billâh.* [In the name of Allah, I rely upon Allah; there is no might and no power except in Allah.]" (from a sound hadith recorded by Abu Dâwood and at-Tirmidhi)

الَّهُمَّ إِنِّي أَعُوذُ بِكَ أَنْ أَضِلَّ، أَوْ أُضَلَّ، أَوْ أَزِلَّ، أَوْ أُزَلَّ، أَوْ أَظْلِمَ، أَوْ أُظْلَمَ، أَوْ أَجْهَلَ، أَوْ يُجْهَلَ عَلَيَّ

Say, "*Allâhumma innee a'oodhu bika an aḍilla, aw uḍalla, aw azilla, aw uzalla, aw adhlima, aw udhlama, aw ajhala aw yujhala 'alayya.* [O Allah, I take refuge with You lest I should stray or be led astray, or slip or be tripped, or oppress or be oppressed, or behave foolishly or be treated foolishly.]" (from a sound hadith recorded by Abu Dâwood, at-Tirmidhi, Ibn Mâjah and an-Nasâ'i)

When going to the mosque

اللَّهُمَّ اجْعَلْ فِي قَلْبِي نُوراً، وَفِي لِسَانِي نُوراً، وَفِي سَمْعِي نُوراً، وَفِي بَصَرِي نُوراً، وَمِنْ فَوْقِي نُوراً، وَمِنْ تَحْتِي نُوراً، وَعَنْ يَمِينِي نُوراً، وَعَنْ شِمَالِي نُوراً، وَمِن أَمَامِي نُوراً، وَمِنْ خَلْفِي نُوراً، وَاجْعَلْ فِي نَفْسِي

نُوراً، وَأَعْظِمْ لِي نُوراً، وَعَظِّمْ لِي نُوراً، وِاجْعَلْ لِي نُوراً، وِاجْعَلْنِي نُوراً،
اللَّهُمَّ أَعْطِنِي نُوراً، وِاجْعَلْ فِي عَصَبِي نُوراً، وَفِي لَحْمِي نُوراً،
وَفِي دَمِي نُوراً، وَفِي شَعْرِي نُوراً، وَفِي بَشَرِي نُوراً

Say, "*Allâhummaj'al fee qalbee nooran, wa fee lisânee nooran, wa fee sam'ee nooran, wa fee baṣaree nooran, wa min fawqee nooran, wa min taḥtee nooran, wa 'an yameenee nooran, wa 'an shimâlee nooran, wa min amâmee nooran, wa min khalfee nooran, waj'al fee nafsee nooran, waj'al fee nafsee nooran, wa a'<u>dh</u>im lee nooran, wa 'adh-dhim lee nooran, waj'al lee nooran, waj'alnee nooran. Allâhumma a'ṭinee nooran, waj'al fee 'aṣabee nooran wa fee laḥmee nooran, wa fee damee nooran, wa fee sha'ree nooran, wa fee basharee nooran.* [O Allah, place within my heart light, and upon my tongue light, and within my ears light, and within my sight light, and above me light and below me light and to my right light and to my left light and before me light and behind me light. Place in my soul light. Magnify for me light, and amplify for me light. Make for me light and make me a light. O Allah, grant me light, and place light in my nerves, and in my body light and in my blood light and in my hair light and in my skin light.]" (Bukhari and Muslim)

When entering the mosque

أَعُوذُ بِاللَّهِ الْعَظِيمِ، وَبِوَجْهِهِ الْكَرِيمِ، وَسُلْطَانِهِ الْقَدِيمِ،
مِنَ الشَّيْطَانِ الرَّجِيمِ. [بِسْمِ اللَّهِ، وَالصَّلَاةُ وَالسَّلَامُ عَلَى رَسُولِ اللَّهِ]
اللَّهُمَّ افْتَحْ لِي أَبْوَابَ رَحْمَتِكَ.

Say, "*A'oodhu billâhil-'Aḏheem, wa bi-wajhihil-kareem, wa sulṭânihil-qadeemi minash-shayṭânir-rajeem, [bismillâhi, waṣṣalâtu wassalâmu 'alâ Rasoolillâh.] Allâhum-maftaḥ lee abwâba raḥmatik.*

[I seek refuge in Allah the Almighty, by His noble Face and by His eternal authority, from the accursed Satan.[55] (In the name of Allah, and prayers[56] and peace be upon the Messenger of Allah.[57]) O Allah, open for me the doors of Your mercy.]"[58]

When leaving the mosque

بِسْمِ اللَّهِ، وَالصَّلَاةُ وَالسَّلَامُ عَلَى رَسُولِ اللَّهِ، اللَّهُمَّ إِنِّي أَسْأَلُكَ مِنْ فَضْلِكَ، اللَّهُمَّ اعْصِمْنِي مِنَ الشَّيْطَانِ الرَّجِيمِ

Say, "*Bismillâhi wassalâtu wassalâmu 'alâ rasoolillâhi, Allâhumma innee asaluka min faḍlika. Allâhumma'ṣimnee minash-shaytânir-rajeem.* [In the name of Allah, and prayers and peace be upon the Messenger of Allah. O Allah! I seek Your grace and favour. O Allah! Protect me from the accursed devil.]"

After leaving the mosque, the Prophet (ﷺ) would recite certain phrases, remembering and glorifying Allah (ﷻ). The time after dawn was also one of the private times when he would sometimes make love to one of his wives. Therefore, it is part of the Sunnah to make the morning remembrances and to have sexual intimacy with one's wife after the dawn prayer. There are many remembrances that were made by the Prophet (ﷺ) in the morning. To keep this section from being too lengthy, I have included them in an appendix at the end of the book.

After the sun rose, the Prophet (ﷺ) would pray the optional mid-morning prayer, and then he (ﷺ) would go to his work, which would end when the sun reached its zenith. Right after that, the

---

[55] From a sound hadith recorded by Abu Dâwood
[56] From a reliable hadith recorded by Ibn as-Sunni
[57] From a sound hadith recorded by Abu Dâwood
[58] Muslim

Prophet (ﷺ) would return home and perform four units of optional prayers.

When you enter the house

بِسْمِ اللَّهِ وَلَجْنَا، وَبِسْمِ اللَّهِ خَرَجْنَا، وَعَلَى رَبِّنَا تَوَكَّلْنَا

Say, "*Bismillâhi walajnâ, wa bismillâhi kharajnâ, wa 'alâ rabbanâ tawakkalnâ.* [In the name of Allah we enter, and in His name we come out, and upon our Lord we trust and depend.]" (from a sound hadith recorded by Abu Dâwood)

Next, he would go to the mosque and lead the noon prayer; then he would return home and perform four units of optional prayer in the house. After that, there would be private time with his wife when they could have sexual intimacy if they chose to.[59]

Before you take your clothes off

بِسْمِ اللَّهِ

Say, "*Bismillâh.* [In the name of Allah.]" (from a sound hadith recorded by at-Tirmidhi)

Before you engage in sexual intercourse

بِسْمِ اللَّهِ اللَّهُمَّ جَنِّبْنَا الشَّيْطَانَ وجَنِّبِ الشَّيْطَانَ مَا رَزَقْتَنَا.

---

[59] The Sharia gives the husband and wife three times during the day when their children, parents, and friends are supposed to give them privacy. They should not visit them or knock on their doors unless it is an emergency. These times are after the dawn prayer, after the evening prayer, and right after the noon prayer. These are times where the husband and wife have time for themselves to have physical, emotional, and/or sexual intimacy.

Say, *"Bismillâhillâhumma jannibnash-shaytâna wa jannibish-shaytâna mâ razaqtanâ.* [In the name of Allah, keep us away from Satan, and keep him away from what You have bestowed upon us.]" (Bukhari and Muslim)

After private time with his wife, the Prophet (ﷺ) would take a nap. (In periods of extreme heat — which we in the West might call the 'dog days of summer' — the Prophet (ﷺ) would delay the prayer towards the end of its time until the temperature cooled off some. On these days, he would take his nap before the noon prayer.)

Dhikr (remembrances of Allah) to be said before sleeping

بِاسْمِكَ رَبِّي وَضَعْتُ جَنْبِي، وَبِكَ أَرْفَعُهُ، فَإِنْ أَمْسَكْتَ نَفْسِي فَارْحَمْهَا، وَإِنْ أَرْسَلْتَهَا فَاحْفَظْهَا، بِمَا تَحْفَظُ بِهِ عِبَادَكَ الصَّالِحِينَ

«Abu Hurayrah (ﷺ) narrated that the Prophet (ﷺ) said: When any of you goes to bed, he should shake out and brush off the bedding, even inside, because he does not know what followed in his absence, and say: *Bismika Rabbee wada'tu janbee, wa bika arfa'uhu, fa-in amsakta nafsee farhamhâ, wa in arsaltahâ fâhfadh-hâ, bimâ tahfadhu bihi 'ibâdaka as-sâliheen.* [In Your name, O Lord, I lay myself down, and in Your name I shall get up. So if You hold my soul, then be merciful to it, but if You send it back, then preserve it as You preserve Your pious slaves.]» (Muslim)

He (ﷺ) led the afternoon prayer in the mosque when it was time. After that, he (ﷺ) would repeat the remembrances that he recited in the morning. When the Prophet (ﷺ) was not leading the prayer, during the time between his nap and the sunset, he would help one of his wives (may Allah be pleased with them) with the housework. He (ﷺ) also would take the time on various days to visit the sick, entertain guests, spend time with his family, play with his grandchildren (may Allah be pleased with them), eat a meal, teach classes, make supplications, and do other good deeds.

When the sun set, he (ﷺ) would go to the mosque to lead the sunset prayer. Afterwards, he (ﷺ) would return home and pray two units of optional prayer. He would not go out at night except when he led the evening prayer; after that, he (ﷺ) would return home and pray two units of optional prayer in his house. Then he (ﷺ) would spend private time with one of his wives (may Allah be pleased with them). He (ﷺ) would recite the remembrances before sleeping. He (ﷺ) would sleep two-thirds of the night, then wake up during the last third of the night and pray eleven long units of the optional late night prayer. In that prayer, he would recite a great deal of Qur'an, glorify Allah (ﷻ) through phrases of remembrance, and supplicate to Allah for his needs.

The Unseen World and its Effects on our Reality

$\mathcal{A}$ ll problems have layers of reality. There are the physical realities (that is, the problems themselves), the spiritual realities (which manifest themselves in the world of the angels and the jinn), and the ultimate reality [Allah (ﷻ), Who is al-Ḥaqq], which we understand through our belief in tawḥeed. In order to solve our problems, we need to understand the layers of our problems, so that we can fight them at all levels.

Every event that happens in the world has three causes simultaneously: a material/scientific cause, a spiritual cause, and an ultimate cause.

❨Do you not see that Allah drives clouds? Then He brings them together, then He makes them into a mass, and you see the rain emerge from within it...❩ *(Qur'an 24: 43)*

The previous verse gave a scientific and material cause for the rain. The next verse gives a spiritual cause.

❨And those [angels] who drive [the clouds].❩ *(Qur'an 37: 2)*

Rain is caused by the water cycle (the material reality). The water cycle is commanded and regulated by angels (peace be upon them) that Allah (ﷻ) commanded to regulate them (the spiritual reality). The true reality and true cause behind everything is Allah (ﷻ) (al-Ḥaqq — the Ultimate Reality). Allah is the power behind everything that moves. Nothing can move without Allah (ﷻ) empowering it to move.

Likewise, illness is caused by bacterial microbes, viruses, chemical imbalances, or abnormal cell growths; this is the material reality. The jinn have the power to spread bacteria and viruses, and to cause chemical imbalances as well; this can sometimes be the spiritual reality. Yet the ultimate reality is Allah (ﷻ), as all diseases and cures originate from Him (ﷻ).

Just like the physical and spiritual worlds have layers of reality, human beings have layers as well. Every human being has a *nafs*, a *rooh*, and a *qalb*. The nafs is your lower self, which inclines towards fulfilling all of your worldly and material desires. The rooh is your higher self, which inclines towards fulfilling the angelic realm and closeness to God. The qalb is your spiritual heart; it turns towards whichever side is stronger.

In the spiritual realm, the angels (peace be upon them) encourage you to do deeds that the Sharia considers to be good. As you do more good deeds, more angels will accompany you; when more angels accompany you, you will find it easier to perform good deeds, and you will find it harder to sin. You also may find that you think of more things to ask Allah (ﷻ) for.

In the spiritual realm, the satanic beings communicate to you by whispering to your lower self. They encourage you to do whatever you want to do, regardless of what the Sharia says about it. If you do more bad deeds, the number of satans with you will increase, while the number of angels will decrease.

Your heart will incline towards whichever influence in your life is stronger. This is determined by how you spend your time, as well as what your companions do with their time.

The places Angels (ﷺ) inhabit

The Mosque

«The Prophet (ﷺ) said: Then when he enters the mosque, he is in (the state of) prayer as long as it is the only thing keeping him from leaving (in other words, the only reason why he is staying in the mosque is to wait for the next prayer). The angels send prayers upon one of you as long as he is in the seat (spot) that he prayed in; they say: O Allah, have mercy on him; O Allah, forgive him; Allah, accept his repentance, as long as he does not harm anyone (with speech or deed) while he is in it, and as long as he does not nullify his state of purity (for instance, by passing wind and the like).» (a sound hadith recorded by Abu Dâwood)

«The Prophet (ﷺ) said: You are constantly being frequented (in successive shifts) by angels at night and angels during the day, and they gather together during the afternoon prayer and during the dawn prayer.» (Bukhari and Muslim) This is why these two prayers are the greatest of all prayers. Abu Hurayrah (ﷺ) noted that Allah (ﷻ) says:

❨Establish prayer at the decline of the sun [from its meridian] until the darkness of the night and [also] the Qur'an of dawn. Indeed, the recitation of dawn is ever witnessed.❩   *(Qur'an 17: 78)*

«Abu Hurayrah (ﷺ) reported that the Messenger of Allah (ﷺ) said: The angels supplicate in favour of one of you as long as he remains in the place where he has performed prayer, in a state of purity. They (the angels) say: O Allah! Forgive him, O Allah! Have mercy on him.» (Bukhari)

Places where people are remembering Allah or reciting the Qur'an

«Ibn 'Umar (ﷺ) reported that the Prophet (ﷺ) said: When you pass by the gardens of paradise, avail yourselves of them. The Companions asked: What are the gardens of paradise, O Messenger of Allah? He replied: The circles of remembrance of Allah (ﷻ).» (a reliable hadith recorded by at-Tirmidhi and Aḥmad)

«Abu Hurayrah (ﷺ) and Abu Saʿeed al-Khudri (ﷺ) reported: The Messenger of Allah (ﷺ) said: When a group of people assembles for the remembrance of Allah, the angels surround them (with their wings), (Allah's) mercy envelops them, tranquility descends upon them, and Allah (ﷺ) makes a mention of them before those who are near Him.» (Muslim)

«Abu Hurayrah (ﷺ) reported: The Messenger of Allah (ﷺ) said: Allah (ﷺ) has teams of angels who go about on the roads seeking those who remember Allah (ﷺ). When they find some people remembering Allah, they call to one another and say: Come to what you are looking for, and they surround them with their wings until the space between them and the lowest sky is fully covered. Allah asks them (although He is best informed about everything): What are my slaves saying? They say: They are declaring Your Perfectness, praising, remembering the Greatness and Majesty of Allah. He (ﷺ) asks: Have they seen Me? They reply: No, indeed, they have not seen You. He (ﷺ) asks: How would they act if they were to see Me? Thereupon they reply: If they were to see You, they would engage more earnestly in worshipping and glorifying You and would extol You more. He (ﷺ) says: What do they beg of Me? They say: They beg You for Your paradise. Allah (ﷺ) says: Have they seen My paradise? They say: No, our Lord. He (ﷺ) says: How would they act if they were to see My paradise? They reply: Were they to see it, they would more intensely yearn for it. The angels say: They seek Your protection. He (ﷺ) asks: Against what do they seek My protection? The angels say: Our Lord, from the fire of hell. Allah (ﷺ) says: Have they seen the fire of hell? They say: No, by Your honour, they have not seen it. He (ﷺ) says: How would they act if they were to see My Fire? They say: If they were to see it, they would be more earnest in being away from it and fearing it. They beg of You forgiveness. He (ﷺ) says: I call you to witness that I hereby grant pardon to them and confer upon them what they ask for, and grant them protection against what they seek protection from. One of the angels says: Our Lord, there is amongst them such and such slave who does not belong to the assembly of those who are participating in Your remembrance. He passed by them and sat down with them. He (ﷺ) says: I also grant him pardon because they are the people by virtue of whom their associates will not be unfortunate.» (Bukhari and Muslim)

Places where people are seeking and spreading religious/spiritual knowledge

«Abud-Dardâ' (ﷺ) narrated that the Messenger of Allah (ﷺ) said: He who treads a path in search of knowledge, Allah (ﷺ) will direct him to tread a path from the paths of paradise. The angels lower their wings for the student of knowledge in approval of what he does. All in the heavens and earth, and the fish in the depth of the water, seek forgiveness for the scholar, and the superiority of the scholar over the worshipper is like the superiority of the full moon at night over the rest of the stars. Verily, the scholars are the heirs to the prophets. Verily, the prophets did not bequeath dinars or dirhams. All they left behind was knowledge, so whoever takes it has indeed acquired a huge fortune.» (a sound hadith recorded by Abu Dâwood, at-Tirmidhi, Ibn Mâjah, ad-Darimi, and Ibn Hibbân)

«Safwân ibn 'Assâl (ﷺ) said: I came to the Prophet (ﷺ) while he was reclining on a red coat (in the mosque), and I said to him: O Messenger of Allah! I came to seek knowledge. He said: Welcome, knowledge seeker! Indeed, the angels surround the knowledge seeker with their wings; then they pile on top of each other until they reach the lower heaven out of their love of what he is seeking.» (a sound hadith recorded by Ahmad and at-Tabarâni)

«Abu Hurayrah (ﷺ) reported that the Messenger of Allah (ﷺ) said: Any group of people that assembles in one of the houses of Allah (ﷺ) to study the Qur'an, tranquility will descend upon them, mercy will engulf them, angels will surround them and Allah will make mention of them to those (angels) in His proximity.» (Muslim)

Clean places

«Abu Mâlik al-Ash'ari (ﷺ) reported that the Messenger of Allah (ﷺ) said: Cleanliness is half of faith, and *alhamdulillâh* (praise be to Allah) fills the scale, and *Subhânallâh* (glory be to Allah) and *alhamdulillâh* (praise be to Allah) fill up what is between the heavens and the earth, and prayer is a light, and charity is proof (of one's faith), and endurance is a brightness, and the Qur'an is a proof on your behalf or against you. All men go out early in the morning and sell themselves, thereby setting themselves free or destroying themselves. *(Muslim)*

Where the Angels do not go

Ibn 'Abbâs (ﷺ) reported that the Messenger of Allah (ﷺ) said: «Angels do not enter a house in which there is a dog or a picture.» (Muslim) This applies to all angels except three kinds: the guardian angels, the angels that write down one's deeds, and the angels of death.

Satan and the Jinn

Satan has certain strengths and weaknesses. Allah (ﷺ) created him and his followers from amongst jinn and human beings, in order to test us. In this section, we will learn more about Satan and ways of protecting ourselves from him and the jinn.

Satan tries to make you forget what you are supposed to do

❨He said, 'Did you see when we retired to the rock? Indeed, I forgot [there] the fish. And none made me forget it except Satan — that I should mention it. And it took its course into the sea amazingly.'❩

(Qur'an 18: 63)

❨And when you see those who engage in [offensive] discourse concerning Our verses, then turn away from them until they enter into another conversation. And if Satan should cause you to forget, then do not remain after the reminder with the wrongdoing people.❩

(Qur'an 6: 68)

Satan whispers false promises and leaves you in your hour of need

❨...But Satan does not promise them except delusion.❩

(Qur'an 17: 64)

❨And [remember] when Satan made their deeds pleasing to them and said: No one can overcome you today from among the people, and indeed, I am your protector. But when the two armies sighted each other, he turned on his heels and said: Indeed, I am disassociated from you. Indeed, I see what you do not see; indeed I fear Allah. And Allah is severe in penalty.❩

(Qur'an 8: 48)

Satan answers some prayers when you pray to other than God, so that you keep saying them

❨They call upon instead of Him none but female [deities], and they [actually] call upon none but a rebellious Satan.❩ *(Qur'an 4: 117)*

Satan tries to replace the laws of Allah with superstitions

❨'...And I will mislead them, and I will arouse in them [sinful] desires, and I will command them so they will slit the ears of cattle, and I will command them so they will change the creation of Allah.' And whoever takes Satan as an ally instead of Allah has certainly sustained a clear loss. Satan promises them and arouses desire in them. But Satan does not promise them except delusion.❩

(Qur'an 4: 119-120)

Satan accesses you through alcohol and gambling

❨O you who have believed, indeed, intoxicants, gambling, [sacrificing on] stone altars [to other than Allah], and divining arrows are but defilement from the work of Satan, so avoid it that you may be successful. Satan only wants to cause between you animosity and hatred through intoxicants and gambling and to avert you from the remembrance of Allah and from prayer. So will you not desist?❩

(Qur'an 5: 90-91)

Satan makes evil look good

❨I found her and her people prostrating to the sun instead of Allah, and Satan has made their deeds pleasing to them and averted them from [His] way, so they are not guided.❩   *(Qur'an 27: 24)*

❨By Allah, We did certainly send [messengers] to nations before you, but Satan made their deeds attractive to them. And he is the disbelievers' ally today [as well], and they will have a painful punishment.❩   *(Qur'an 16: 63)*

Satan tries to divide people and cause conflicts between them

❲And tell My servants to say that which is best. Indeed, Satan induces [dissension] among them. Indeed Satan is ever, to mankind, a clear enemy.❳   *(Qur'an 17: 53)*

Satan threatens you with poverty

❲Satan threatens you with poverty and orders you to immorality...❳
(Qur'an 2: 268)

How to combat Satan

Make dhikr when evil thoughts come into your head

❲Indeed, those who fear Allah — when an impulse touches them from Satan, they remember [Him] and at once they have insight.❳
(Qur'an 7: 201)

«Abu Hurayrah (رضي الله عنه) narrated that the Messenger of Allah (ﷺ) said: Whoever says *lâ ilâha illâ Allâh waḥdahu lâ shareeka lahu, lahul mulku wa lahul ḥamdu, wa Huwa 'alâ kulli shay'in Qadeer* (There is none worthy of worship other than Allah alone, who has no partner; His is the dominion and His is the praise, and He is All-Powerful over all things) one hundred times daily will get the reward for freeing ten captives; he or she will get one hundred blessings, one hundred mistakes will be wiped out, and it will be a protection for him or her from Satan all that day until the night. No one will get a better reward except one who did more than that.» (Bukhari and Muslim)

Try to maintain ritual purity all day, and rinse your nose three times after waking up

Abu Hurayrah (ﷺ) narrated that the Prophet (ﷺ) said: «If any one of you gets up from sleep and performs ablution, he should wash his nose by putting water in it and then blowing it out three times, because Satan has stayed in the upper part of his nose all the night.» (Bukhari)

Do not go out at nightfall unless it is necessary, and mention the name of Allah at your door and over your food

«Jâbir ibn 'Abdullah (ﷺ) narrated that the Apostle of Allah (ﷺ) said: When night falls (or it is evening), keep your children close to you, for the devils spread out at that time. After an hour of the night elapses, you can let them free. Close the doors and mention the name of Allah (ﷺ), for Satan does not open a closed door.» (Bukhari and Muslim)

«Jâbir (ﷺ) said that he heard the Prophet (ﷺ) say: When a man enters his house and remembers Allah the Exalted upon entering and before eating, Satan says: There is no place for you to spend the night, and there is no supper for you. When he enters the house and does not remember Allah (ﷺ), Satan says: You have found a place to spend the night. When he does not remember Allah (ﷺ) upon eating his food, Satan says: You have found a place to stay and some supper.» (Muslim)

«Ḥudhayfah (ﷺ) reported: When we attended a meal with the Messenger of Allah (ﷺ), we would not stretch forth our hands towards the food until he (ﷺ) would start eating first. Once we were with him when a little girl rushed in as if someone was compelling her. She was about to lay her hand on the food when the Messenger of Allah (ﷻ) caught her hand. Then a Bedouin came in, rushing as if someone were pushing him. He (ﷺ) caught his hand also and said: Satan considers that food lawful for himself on whom the name of Allah (ﷻ) is not mentioned. He (Satan) brought this girl to make the food lawful for him through her, but I caught her hand. Then he brought the Bedouin to make it lawful through him, but I caught his hand too. By Him in Whose Hand my soul is, now Satan's hand is in my grasp along with their hands. Then he mentioned the name of Allah (ﷻ) and began to eat.» (Muslim, Abu Dâwood and an-Nasâ'i)

Recite the last two chapters of the Qur'an

«Abu Sa'eed al-Khudri (ﷺ) reported: The Messenger of Allah (ﷺ) used to seek protection against the evil of jinn and the evil eyes until soorat al-Falaq and soorat an-Nâs [the last two chapters of the Qur'an] were revealed. After they were revealed, he took to them for seeking the protection of Allah (ﷻ) and left everything besides them.» (a sound hadith recorded by at-Tirmidhi)

Recite the second chapter of the Qur'an in your home

Abu Hurayrah (ﷺ) reported that he heard the Messenger of Allah (ﷺ) say: «Do not turn your houses into graveyards. Satan runs away from the house in which soorat al-Baqarah [the second chapter of the Qur'an] is recited.» (Muslim)

The Prophet (ﷺ) said: «The house in which [soorat] al-Baqarah is recited is not approached by Satan.» (Muslim)

You can also have Qur'an recited in your home by using CDs, cassettes, computer programs and the like.

When waking from a nightmare

Jâbir (ﷺ) narrated that the Messenger of Allah (ﷺ) said: «When someone sees unpleasant dreams, he should spit to his left three times and seek refuge in Allah (ﷻ) from the outcast Satan. Then he should turn and sleep on his other side.» (Muslim, Abu Dâwood, an-Nasâ'i and Ibn Mâjah)

Recite Ayat-ul-Kursi (Qur'an 2: 255)

«Abu Hurayrah (﵁) reported: The Messenger of Allah (ﷺ) put me in charge of the charity of Ramadan. Somebody came to me and began to take away handfuls of the foodstuff. I caught him and said: By Allah, I must take you to the Messenger of Allah (ﷺ). He said: I am a needy man with a large family, and so I have a pressing need. I let him go. When I saw the Messenger of Allah (ﷺ) the next morning, he asked me: O Abu Hurayrah! What did your captive do last night? I said: O Messenger of Allah! He complained of a pressing need and a big family. I felt pity for him, so I let him go. He (ﷺ) said: He told you a lie, and he will return. I was sure, according to the saying of the Messenger of Allah (ﷺ), that he would return. I waited for him. He snuck up again and began to steal foodstuff from the charity. I caught him and said: I must take you to the Messenger of Allah (ﷺ). He said: Let go of me. I am a needy man. I have to bear the expenses of a big family. I will not come back. So I took pity on him and let him go. I went at dawn to the Messenger of Allah (ﷺ), who asked me: O Abu Hurayrah! What did your captive do last night? I replied: O Messenger of Allah! He complained of a pressing want and the burden of a big family. I took pity on him, and so I let him go. He (ﷺ) said: He told you a lie, and he will return. (That man) came again to steal the foodstuff. I arrested him and said: I must take you to the Messenger of Allah (ﷺ), and this is the last of three times; you promised that you would not come again, but you did. He said: Let go of me, and I shall teach you some words with which Allah (ﷻ) may benefit you. I asked: What are those words? He replied: When you go to bed, recite *Ayat-ul-Kursi (Qur'an 2: 255)*, for there will be a guardian appointed over you from Allah (ﷻ), and Satan will not be able to approach you until morning. So I let him go. The next morning, the Messenger of Allah (ﷺ) asked me: What did your prisoner do last night? I answered: He promised to teach me some words which he claimed would benefit me before Allah (ﷻ), so I let him go. The Messenger of Allah (ﷺ) asked: What are those words that he taught you? I said: He told me: When you go to bed, recite *Ayat-ul-Kursi* from the beginning to the end. He added: By reciting it, there will be a guardian appointed over you from Allah (ﷻ), who will protect you during the night, and Satan will not be able to come near you until morning. The Messenger of Allah (ﷺ) said: Verily, he has told you the truth although he is a liar. O Abu Hurayrah! Do you know with whom you were speaking for the last three nights? I said: No. He (ﷺ) said: He was Satan.» (Bukhari)

Stick to the body of Muslims

The Prophet (ﷺ) said: «...Stick to the congregation (of Muslims), and avoid division. Satan is with the one person alone but is more likely to avoid the two together. Whosoever wants abundance in paradise should stick to the congregation (of Muslims)...» (a sound hadith recorded by at-Tirmidhi and Ibn Mâjah)

Abud-Dardâ' (ﻬ) reported that he heard the Messenger of Allah (ﷺ) say: «If three men in a village, or in the desert, make no arrangement for prayer in congregation, Satan must have certainly overcome them. So observe prayer in congregation, for the wolf eats up a solitary sheep that strays far from the flock.» (a sound hadith recorded by Abu Dâwood)

Recite the call to prayer and go to the mosque for congregational prayer

«Abu Hurayrah (ﻬ) narrated that Allah's Apostle (ﷺ) said: When the first call to prayer is pronounced, Satan takes to his heels and passes wind with noise during his flight in order not to hear it. When the first call to prayer is completed, he comes back, and again takes to his heels when the second call to prayer is pronounced. After its completion, he returns again until he whispers into the heart of the person (to divert his attention from his prayer) and makes him remember things which he does not recall before the prayer, and that causes him to forget how much he has prayed.» (Bukhari)

«Abu Sufyân (رضى الله عنه) reported it on the authority of Jâbir (رضى الله عنه) that he heard the Apostle of Allah (ﷺ) say: When Satan hears the call to prayer, he runs away to a distance like that of Rauha. Sulaiman said: I asked him about Rauha. He replied: It is at a distance of thirty-six miles from Madinah.» (Muslim)

Seek the protection of Allah (ﷺ) before reciting Qur'an and when one gets angry

❲'When you commence reciting the Qur'an, seek protection from Allah against the accursed Satan.'❳ *(Qur'an 16: 98)*

How to Correctly Enjoin the Right and Forbid the Wrong

*E*arlier in the book, we discussed the importance of commanding people to do good and forbidding people from doing evil. There are also rulings on this matter of enjoining the right and forbidding the wrong, and there is a distinction made between the scholar and the common Muslim.

The scholars are obliged to give their legal opinion on any issue that they have researched and to teach it to the people, regardless of whom they contradict and regardless of whether the issue is obligatory, recommended, permissible, detested, or forbidden. They can command people to do something or forbid people from doing something if they present their evidence, even if there is a difference of opinion among the scholars.

The common Muslim can only enjoin the right and forbid the evil on matters that are agreed upon. For example, he or she can forbid another Muslim from drinking beer, since there is no disagreement on this issue. However, an ordinary Muslim cannot forbid someone from putting the hands on the chest or from leaving them at the side (when rising from the bowing position into the standing position of prayer) because there is a difference of opinion on what the Prophet (ﷺ) did.

What should the regular Muslims do when they see something that they believe to be wrong, but for which they do not have clear evidence (as they would for an issue like drinking beer)? They should do research to find out whether there is a consensus on this question among the scholars of Islam throughout history. If it is agreed upon that the action is forbidden, then they should forbid it. If some scholars say that it is permissible and others say it is forbidden, then they should leave it because it is not their place to forbid it.

If you have the ability to change the evil with your hands or body, you should do so, as long as doing so will not create a greater harm or bring harm to you and your family. If you cannot change it physically, then you should speak out against it, unless you fear that you will cause more harm or bring harm to yourself and your family. If that is the case, then you should just hate the evil in your heart.

You must have a pure intention when giving sincere advice. The Prophet (ﷺ) said: «All actions are by intentions, and every person shall have that which he intended.» (Bukhari and Muslim)

«The Prophet (ﷺ) also said: The religion is sincere advice. We (his Companions) said: To whom? He said: to Allah, His books, His messengers, to the leaders of the Muslims and their common people.» (Muslim)

How can you tell whether you are giving advice sincerely for the sake of Allah? If you are sincere, you realize that people may choose not to take the advice, so if they do not listen, you move on. If you are giving advice for the sake of your nafs, you may become angry, defensive, argumentative, or pushy with the people that you are trying to guide. If this is the case, then you need to follow the advice for the disease of desiring esteem in the eyes of others. Next, you must follow the advice of the Qur'an:

❝Say: Produce your proof, if you should be truthful.❞

(Qur'an 27: 64)

If you plan on giving advice, bring the verses and hadiths that prove your point. Be prepared for the possibility that the other person may have verses and hadiths that prove a different point. If this is the case, do not get involved in arguments over religious matters unless the two of you know each other, have mutual respect for one another, and are both open to being wrong.

Follow the Sunnah of the Prophet (ﷺ) in your dealings. Study how he (ﷺ) gave advice and enjoined the right and forbade the wrong, and follow his way.

The Problems of Backbiting, Spying, and Not Verifying Information

$\mathcal{T}$his chapter is of the utmost importance to Muslims because these are the most common sins that most believers commit. Some commit them due to a personal weakness, while others commit them due to the fact that they do not understand what each one means. After reading this chapter, you should have an understanding of what these three sins are, so that you can get on the path of removing them from your life.

The Qur'an teaches us how to treat other Muslims and non-Muslims. First, we should not seek to find the faults of others. If you search hard enough, you will find something wrong with just about everyone. The Qur'an states:

❨...And do not spy or backbite each other...❩[60]   *(Qur'an 49: 12)*

We should be focusing on eliminating our own faults. If we are not doing so, then we are destroying our own souls by neglecting them while we try to find out what is wrong with the soul of someone else. Next, the Qur'an states:

❨O you who have believed, if there comes to you a disobedient one with information, investigate, lest you harm a people out of ignorance and become, over what you have done, regretful.❩ *(Qur'an 49: 6)*

The Arabic word, translated here as 'a disobedient one', is *fâsiq*, which literally means an evildoer. According to the explanation of this particular verse, though, the word 'fâsiq' here refers to 'people of doubtful character, (or) those whose honesty has

---

[60] This does not apply when one is engaged in war.

not yet been proven, or known sinners'.[61] The verse was revealed about a noble Companion (ﷺ) who had made a bad mistake that had serious consequences for the community; nevertheless, he was not a consistent evildoer.

Before you spread any information, you should verify it. If you hear something about a person, go to him or her and confirm it before spreading that information. This applies no matter who told you, because even the most righteous person you know may be incorrect about another person and pass on false information. How many lives have been hurt, destroyed, or ended because people have unintentionally passed on false information? You may actually cause such damage by your action. Would you want to face Allah (ﷻ) on the Day of Judgment having spread a rumor that destroyed someone's life, only to find out that it was not even true?

Consider how you would feel if you were on the other side. Would you want people to spread information about you without trying to verify it with you first? Imagine that everyone in a community now believed something about you that was not true, because no one bothered to come and ask you about it. Treat other people as you would want them to treat you.

During the time of the first three generations, people lived in close-knit communities. People living in the same neighbourhood all knew each other, and they knew each other's condition as well. A person's reputation could easily be ruined. If anyone lied publicly, he or she would be known to be a liar from that point on. In the modern world, many of us live further apart, and we are distracted by television, the Internet, homework, video games, sports, iPod portable media players and the like. Therefore, it is extremely

---

[61] Philips, Bilal. *Tafseer of Soorat al-Ḥujurât.* Riyadh: International Islamic Publishing House, 2006, p. 94.

difficult to know who is internally truthful despite their external piety and religiosity. In these trying times, it is best for us to err on the side of caution and check anyone's story, no matter how pious the person appears to be. In my short life, I have personally witnessed very religious people (who were considered trustworthy) aid in the destruction of another Muslim's reputation simply because they did not go back and ask that Muslim for his side of the story. They heard something about a Muslim and passed it on to another Muslim, who passed it on to another Muslim — and they all turned out to be wrong because they did not go back and verify it with that person. We have an example of this when some hypocrites accused our mother 'Ā'ishah (رضي الله عنها) of adultery. Word spread around the Muslim community, and it took a verse from the Qur'an to restore her reputation. In these days, no verse is going to come down to restore our reputations, so we need to be extra careful about what we say or believe, and we need to be doubly careful to verify it.

Many people fall into this trap when talking about politics, when they recount what they heard on the news or read in the newspapers. Others go to the further extreme of relating this to some British, Masonic, or Jewish conspiracy theory for which they have no real proof whatsoever. All they have is conjecture. Islam teaches us that a person who narrates whatever he hears is not a truly trustworthy person. Muslims should not relay any information unless they know it firsthand. Even then, they should only relay information that is beneficial and permissible.

The Qur'an compares backbiting to cannibalism. Picture yourself eating a raw carcass of a human being, because this is what you are doing.

❨O you who have believed, avoid much [negative] assumption. Indeed, some assumption is sin. And do not spy or backbite each other. Would one of you like to eat the flesh of his brother when dead? You would detest it. And fear Allah; indeed, Allah is Accepting of repentance and Merciful.» *(Qur'an 49: 12)*

Backbiting means saying something about others, behind their backs, which they would not like to have said about them — even if it is true.

«Abu Hurayrah (ﷺ) narrated: The Messenger of Allah (ﷺ) said: Do you know backbiting? They said: Allah and His messenger know best. He said: When you speak about your brother what he would dislike, it is backbiting. Someone asked: What if my brother is as I say? The Messenger of Allah (ﷺ): If he is as you say, you have been backbiting; if he is not as you say, you have slandered him.» (Muslim)

If you engage in backbiting, reflect on the hadith of the truly bankrupt person. «The Messenger of Allah (ﷺ) said: Do you know who is bankrupt? They — the Companions — said: A bankrupt person is the one who has neither dirham (money) nor wealth. The Prophet (ﷺ) said: The bankrupt person among my followers is the one who would come on the Day of Judgment with prayers, fasting, and zakâh; but he would have offended one person, slandered another, devoured others' wealth, shed the blood of this person, and hit that person. (Consequently) his rewards will be distributed to all of them, and when he loses all his rewards before their accounts are fulfilled, then their sins will be taken and cast upon him, and he will be thrown into the hellfire.» (Muslim)

Think about all of the prayers, fasting, charity, and other good deeds you did in your life. The person you just talked about now has a right to take from your good deeds on the Day of Judgment. Can you afford that? Is it worth it? Reflect on this before you talk about others. Also, try to live up to this hadith: «He who believes in Allah (ﷺ) and the Last Day, let him say what is good or be silent.»

(Bukhari and Muslim) In our culture, we have a similar saying: "If you have nothing nice to say, don't say anything at all."

There is an exercise some scholars recommended to cure one from backbiting. Carry a notepad with you. Every time you backbite, write down what you said, when you said it, where you said it, and whom you were talking to. You may begin to notice a pattern after a week. You may find that you only backbite when you hang out with Zayd or Layla. That will teach you that you have to be extra careful guarding your tongue when you are around Zayd or Layla.

However, there are three occasions when backbiting is permissible. If someone is inquiring about the character of a person for a possible marriage or a business partnership, and you have witnessed firsthand that the person under consideration is morally corrupt, then you must tell the one who is asking. However, you can only relate information that you have seen personally. Also, if you are called to testify in court, you must tell the truth.

Solving the Problems Committed by the Seven Limbs

Our problems are rooted in sins. Sins are manifested on the seven limbs, which may refer to a physical or spiritual nature. This chapter contains exercises developed by our predecessors to help us kick the habits of sin from the seven areas we use to commit sins.

Exercises for the private parts

For forty days straight, give up fornication, adultery, and being in a room alone with an unrelated woman. If you can do it for forty days, you can do it for life.

Exercises for the hands

For forty days straight, give up all the ways that you can harm other human beings with your hands, such as stealing and fighting (except as necessary in self-defense, martial arts class, disciplining your children, or other similar situations). If you can do it for forty days, you can do it for life.

Exercises for the feet

For forty days straight, give up walking or driving to anywhere that you may commit sins. If you can do it for forty days, you can do it for life.

Exercises for the stomach

For forty days straight, give up eating pork, drinking alcohol, and accumulating wealth through interest, gambling, or any other forbidden means. If you can do it for forty days, you can do it for life.

Exercises for the ears

For forty days straight, give up listening to backbiting, slander, spying, and any music or television programs that promote sins. If you can do it for forty days, you can do it for life.

Exercises for the tongue

For forty days straight, give up lying (except in situations when it is permissible, when you are trying to protect someone from physical or mental danger or to reconcile two people who are quarreling), backbiting, slander, gossip, arguing, being nosy and not minding your own business. If you can do it for forty days, you can do it for life.

Exercises for the eyes

For forty days, give up looking lustfully at members of the opposite sex, watching other people sin or being in their environments, or watching television programs that show people committing sins. If you can do it for forty days, you can do it for life.

The Prophecies of the Prophet (ﷺ) Regarding the Causes of and Remedies for the Problems of the Ummah

The Prophet (ﷺ) predicted many of the problems that we face today.[62] In some cases, he (ﷺ) also informed us of the reasons why these problems would occur. This chapter will help us understand the causes and effects of our global problems. This information should increase our faith, soften our hearts and encourage us to solve the problems in our lives, while there is still time.

In the famous hadith of Jibreel (عليه السلام), the Prophet (ﷺ) mentioned the signs of the Day of Judgment as part of the religion, after mentioning the pillars of Islam, the beliefs that make up the Islamic creed, and the perfection of worshipping Allah (ﷻ) as if He could see you.

«...He (Jibreel) said: Tell me about the Hour. The Messenger of Allah (ﷺ) said: The one asked about it knows no more than the one asking. He said: Then tell me about its tokens. He (ﷺ) said: That the female slave should give birth to her mistress, and you see poor, naked, barefoot shepherds of sheep and goats competing in making tall buildings...» (Muslim)

---

[62] These prophecies were collected in books written 1,200 years ago. We are translating them literally, without inserting our own interpretations. This is different from those who translate the alleged prophecies of Nostradamus. They deliberately translate the quatrains (stanzas of four lines each) in a way that will imply the meaning that they desire, and then claim that it was an accurate prediction.

These signs, or prophecies, of the Prophet Muhammad (ﷺ) should remind us and help soften our hearts and help us purify ourselves. The signs can be divided into three categories: those that have already taken place, those that are currently happening, and those that have not yet occurred.

Signs that have already taken place

The death of the Prophet (ﷺ)

The Prophet (ﷺ) died in the year 632 CE.

The fire in Ḥijâz

The Prophet (ﷺ) said: «The Hour will not be established until a fire will come out of the land of Ḥijâz, and it will throw light on the necks of camels at Basra.» (Muslim)

The Ḥijâz, a western region of the Arabian Peninsula, includes the cities of Makkah and Madinah. There was a huge fire near Madinah in the year 654 AH/approximately 1256 CE. Accounts from the time state that its glow could be seen in Basra, which is in southern Iraq.

Fighting the Turks

Abu Hurayrah (ﷺ) reported that Allah's Messenger (ﷺ) said: «The Last Hour will not come until the Muslims fight with the Turks — a people whose faces would be (flat and wide) like hammered shields, wearing clothes of hair and walking (with shoes) of hair.» (Muslim)

Scholars tell us that this refers to the invasion of Iraq by the Mongols in 656 AH.

The defeat of the Muslims and the dividing up of Muslim lands

«On the authority of Thawbân: The Prophet (ﷺ) said: The people will soon summon one another to attack you, like people who are eating invite others to share their food. Someone asked: Will that be because of our small numbers at that time? He replied: No, you will be numerous at that time, but you will be froth and scum like that carried down by a torrent (of water), and Allah (ﷻ) will take the fear of you from the breast (hearts) of your enemy and cast *al-wahn* into your hearts. Someone asked: O Messenger of Allah, what is *al-wahn*? He replied: Love of the world and dislike of death.» (a sound hadith recorded by Abu Dâwood and Aḥmad)

This happened fewer than one hundred years ago. After the Ottoman Empire was defeated in World War I, what was left of the Muslim lands was carved up by the Western powers (who had already done this decades before in Southeast Asia and Africa).

Sanctions on Iraq

«Abu Naḍrah reported: We were in the company of Jâbir ibn 'Abdullah, who said that the Prophet (ﷺ) said: It may happen that the people of Iraq may not send their foodstuff and money. We said: Who would be responsible for it? He (ﷺ) said: The non-Arabs would prevent them...» (Muslim)

In 1990, the United Nations Security Council imposed harsh economic sanctions on Iraq; they were not lifted until 2003.

The loss of Palestine, Chechnya, and other Muslim lands and the reasons why the Muslims lost them; the spread of AIDS; and the current state of Muslim and Middle Eastern political affairs

«'Abdullah ibn 'Umar (﷽) narrated: The Prophet (﷽) came to us and said: O Emigrants, you may be afflicted by five things; Allah (﷽) forbid that you should live to see them. If zinâ (fornication, adultery, homosexuality, and the like) should become widespread, you should realize that this has never happened without new diseases befalling the people, which their ancestors never suffered. If people should begin to cheat in weighing out goods (in business), you should realize that this has never happened without drought and famine befalling the people, and their rulers oppressing them. If people should withhold zakâh, you should realize that this has never happened without the rain being stopped from falling; were it not for the animals' sake, it would never rain again. If people should break their covenant with Allah (﷽) and His Messenger (﷽), you should realize that this has never happened without Allah (﷽) sending an enemy against them to take some of their possessions by force. If the leaders do not govern according to the Book of Allah, you should realize that this has never happened without Allah (﷽) making them into groups and making them fight one another.» (a reliable hadith recorded by Ibn Mâjah and al-Hâkim)

This hadith teaches us the reason why the Muslim lands were conquered and taken over by the Israelis, the Romans, the Russians, the Hindus and others. We also learn the correct way to get them back, which is to renew our covenant with Allah (﷽) and His messenger (﷽) by following the teachings of the Prophet (﷽) in our political, spiritual, religious, mental, military, economic and all other affairs. When the Muslims do things the way he did, our lands will come back to us in time, with far less harm than following another methodology would entail.

We can also add the following hadith: «The Prophet (ﷺ) said: Straighten your rows (he said it three times), by Allah either you straighten your rows or Allah (ﷻ) will cause conflict between your hearts.» (a sound hadith recorded by Abu Dâwood and Ibn Ḥibbân)

Signs that are currently happening

For the sake of brevity, I will merely summarize some of the things described by the Prophet (ﷺ) that we see in our world today. You can find more about this in books or on the Internet if you would like to do more research on your own.

The Prophet (ﷺ) said: «Great distances will be traversed in short spans of time.» (a sound hadith recorded by Ahmad)

The Prophet (ﷺ) said: «The Last Hour will not come before time contracts, a year being like a month, a month like a week, a week like a day, a day like an hour, and an hour like the kindling of a fire.» (a sound hadith recorded by at-Tirmidhi)

The Prophet (ﷺ) stated that adultery and pre-marital sex would become open and accepted practices, to the point that they would become the normal thing to do throughout the earth.

«From among the portents of the Hour are the following:...illegal sexual intercourse will prevail...» (Bukhari)

«Only the wicked, who would commit adultery like asses, would survive, and the Last Hour would come to them.» (Muslim)

The Prophet (ﷺ) also told us that many children would be born out of wedlock (of a man and woman who were not married to each other).[63] He (ﷺ) said: «My Ummah shall continue to enjoy

---

[63] In 2007, forty percent of the babies born in the U.S. were born out of=

blessing and safety until children of fornication become widespread among them.» (a reliable hadith recorded by Aḥmad)

He (ﷺ) also told us that religious scholars will die off and that there will not be enough scholars to replace them: «Near the establishment of the Hour, there will be days during which (religious) knowledge will be taken away (vanish) and general ignorance will spread.» (Bukhari)

In a sound hadith recorded by Aḥmad, the Prophet (ﷺ) told us that the marketplaces of the world would come together and that trade would become so widespread that a woman will be forced to help her husband in business.

The Prophet (ﷺ) stated that all over the world, the consumption of intoxicants will be widespread: «From among the portents of the Hour are the following: drinking of alcoholic drinks will prevail...» (Bukhari)

He (ﷺ) said that some Muslims will consider music to be permitted according to Islamic law: «From among my followers there will be some people who will consider illegal sexual intercourse, wearing of silk, drinking of alcoholic beverages and the use of musical instruments as lawful.» (Bukhari)

The Prophet (ﷺ) stated: «Soon there will be people from my Ummah who will drink wine, calling it by other than its real name. There will be instruments of music and singing on their heads. And they will listen to female singers. Allah (ﷻ) will cleave the earth under them and turn others into apes and swine.» (a sound hadith recorded by Ibn Mâjah)

=wedlock, and the figure is more than fifty percent in several European countries. Since the rest of the world usually follows the U.S., this prophecy may be fulfilled very soon.

He (ﷺ) told us that there will be a massive number of people killing each other all over the world. People will start killing without really knowing why they are doing it, and the victims will not know why they are being killed.

«The Hour (Last Day) will not be established until murders will increase.» (Bukhari)

Abu Hurayrah (رضي الله عنه) reported Allah's Messenger (ﷺ) as saying: «By Him in Whose Hand is my life, a time would come when the murderer would not know why he has committed the murder, and the victim would not know why he has been killed.» (Muslim)

The Prophet (ﷺ) told us that people will lose hope and wish they were dead. They will walk by a grave and say that they wish it were them in that grave. (This might mean that clinical depression will increase).

Abu Hurayrah (رضي الله عنه) reported Allah's Messenger (ﷺ) as saying: «The Last Hour would not come until a person would pass by a grave of another person and say: I wish it had been my abode.» (Muslim)

He also told us that women would begin to wear high hairstyles and would wear clothing that allowed men to see the shape of their bodies.

Abu Hurayrah (رضي الله عنه) reported that Allah's Messenger (ﷺ) said: «Two are the types of the denizens of hell that he (ﷺ) had not seen yet: the first possesses whips like the tail of an ox, and they flog people with them; the (second one) where the women are naked in spite of being dressed, who are seduced and seduce others with their hair high like humps. These women will not get into paradise and they will not smell its odor, although its odor can be smelled from a great distance.» (Muslim)

As we read in the hadith of Jibreel (ﷺ) earlier, Middle-Easterners and other agrarian people will leave agriculture and begin to compete in building tall buildings.

«... and you see poor, naked, barefoot shepherds of sheep and goats competing in making tall buildings...» (Muslim)

Terrorist and revolutionary groups amongst the Muslims

The Prophet (ﷺ) foretold the coming of the Kharijites — the terrorists and revolutionaries[64] — and he (ﷺ) said about them: «During the last days, there will appear some young, foolish people who will say the best words, but their faith will not go beyond their throats (in other words, they will have no faith) and will leave their religion as an arrow goes out of the prey.» (Bukhari)

In a sound hadith recorded by an-Nasâ'i, the Prophet Muhammad (ﷺ) stated that if he were alive when they appeared, he would punish them with the punishment of 'Âd (that is, wipe all of them off the face of the earth).

Signs that have not yet occurred

«Abu Naḍrah reported: We were in the company of Jâbir ibn 'Abdullah, who said that the Prophet (ﷺ) said: ...There is a possibility that the people of Syria may not send their money and their foodstuff. We said: Who would be responsible for it? He said: This prevention would be made by the Romans (or the Europeans).» (Muslim)

Prophet Muhammad (ﷺ) said: «The Hour will not take place until there appears a mountain of gold by the Euphrates River. Then

---

[64] See the chapter 'The Problem of Terrorism'

people will fight over it, and out of every hundred persons, ninety-nine will be killed. Every man among them will say: I wish I would be the one saved.» (Muslim)

«Anas ibn Mâlik (�) said: I shall tell you a hadith which I heard from the Messenger of Allah, and which no one will tell you after me. I heard him say: Among the signs of the Hour will be the disappearance of knowledge and the appearance of ignorance. Adultery will be prevalent, and the drinking of wine will be common. The number of men will decrease, and the number of women will increase until there will be fifty women to be looked after by one man.» (Bukhari and Muslim)

The Prophet (ﷺ) said: «Allah will protect two groups against hellfire: One of them will conquer India, and the other will be with Jesus (عليه السلام).» (a sound hadith recorded by Aḥmad)

There will be a major world war with the Romans (Europeans), and Rome will be conquered. The Prophet (ﷺ) said: «You will attack Arabia, and Allah (ﷻ) will enable you to conquer it; then you will attack Persia, and He (ﷻ) will make you conquer it. Then you will attack Rome, and Allah (ﷻ) will enable you to conquer it; then you will attack the *Dajjâl* (Antichrist), and Allah (ﷻ) will enable you to conquer him.» (Muslim)

The re-conquest of Jerusalem, while the city of Madinah is in ruins. «Narrated Mu'âdh ibn Jabal (�): The Prophet (ﷺ) said: The state of Jerusalem will be flourishing when Yathrib [Madinah] is in ruins, the state of Yathrib will be in ruins when the great war comes, the outbreak of the great war will be at the conquest of Constantinople, and the conquest of Constantinople when the Dajjâl comes forth. He (the Prophet) struck his thigh or his shoulder with his hand and said: This is as true as you are here, or as you are sitting (meaning the narrator Mu'âdh ibn Jabal).» (a sound hadith recorded by Abu Dâwood)

Jewish converts to Islam will conquer Istanbul (which was formerly known as Constantinople). «Abu Hurayrah (ﷺ) reported Allah's Apostle (ﷺ) as saying: You have heard about a city where one side of it is on the land, and the other is in the sea (Constantinople). They said: Allah's Messenger, yes. He said: The Last Hour will not come until seventy thousand persons from Bani Isrâ'eel attack it. When they land there, they will neither fight with weapons nor shoot arrows but will only say: There is no god but Allah and Allah is the Greatest, and one side of it will fall. Thawr (one of the narrators) said: I think that he said the part by the side of the ocean. Then they will say for the second time: There is no god but Allah and Allah is the Greatest, and the second side will also fall, and they will say: There is no god but Allah and Allah is the Greatest, and the gates will be opened for them, and they will enter therein. They will be collecting spoils of war and distributing them amongst themselves when a noise will be heard, and it will be said: Verily, Dajjâl has come. Thus they will leave everything there and turn to him.» (Muslim)

The Prophet (ﷺ) said: «The last Hour will not come upon us until the lands of the Arabs are once again pasture lands and filled with rivers.» (Muslim)

The coming of the Mahdi

A descendant of the Prophet (ﷺ) named Muhammad ibn 'Abdullah will be chosen by Allah (ﷺ) and taught all that he needs to be the leader of the Muslims in one night.[65] The Prophet (ﷺ) told us: «The promised Mahdi will be from among my family. Allah (ﷺ) will make the provisions for his emergence within a single night.» (a sound hadith recorded by ibn Mâjah)

---

[65] Until that time, he will not know that he is the Mahdi; he will find out that night.

The Muslims of the world will pledge their allegiance to him as their caliph. Many of the tyrants of the Muslim world will try and stop him, but they will fail. There will be a global Muslim nation, and many of the other nations of the world will gather against it.

Abu Sa'eed al-Khudri (ﷺ) stated that the Messenger of Allah (ﷺ) said: «The Mahdi is of my lineage, with a high forehead and a long, thin, curved nose. He will fill the earth with fairness and justice as it was filled with oppression and injustice, and he will rule for seven years.» (a reliable hadith recorded by at-Tirmidhi)

The emergence of the Dajjâl

Ibn 'Umar (ﷺ) reported that Allah's Messenger (ﷺ) mentioned the Dajjâl in the presence of the people and said: «Allah is not one-eyed; behold that Dajjâl is blind in the right eye, and his eye is like a floating grape.» (Muslim)

«Anas ibn Mâlik (ﷺ) reported that Allah's Messenger (ﷺ) said: Dajjâl is blind in one eye, and there is written between his eyes the word '*Kafir*' (nonbeliever). He then spelled the word as the Arabic equivalent of 'k,f,r', which every Muslim would be able to read.» (Muslim)

Ubâdah ibn aṣ-Ṣâmit (ﷺ) narrated that the Prophet (ﷺ) said: «I have told you so much about the Dajjâl that I am afraid you may not understand. The Antichrist is short, pigeon-toed, woolly-haired, one-eyed, an eye sightless, and neither protruding nor deep-seated. If you are confused about him, know that your Lord is not one-eyed.» (a sound hadith recorded by Abu Dâwood)

He will emerge after a global famine, but he will have plenty of food and water. The minds of the people will be weakened from lack of food and water, so they will be very susceptible to his deception.

«An-Nawwâs ibn Sam'ân (رضي الله عنه) reported that Allah's Messenger (ﷺ) mentioned the Dajjâl one morning. He sometimes described him to be insignificant and sometimes described (his turmoil) as very significant (and we felt) as if he were in the cluster of the date-palm trees. When we went to him (to the Prophet) in the evening, and he read (the signs of fear) in our faces, he said: What is the matter with you? We said: Allah's Messenger, you mentioned the Dajjâl in the morning (sometimes describing him) to be insignificant and sometimes very important, until we began to think as if he were present in some (near) part of the cluster of the date-palm trees. He said: I fear for you in so many other things besides the Dajjâl. If he comes forth while I am among you, I shall contend with him on your behalf, but if he comes forth while I am not among you, a man must contend on his own behalf, and Allah will take care of every Muslim on my behalf (and safeguard him against his evil). He (Dajjâl) will be a young man with twisted, contracted hair and a blind eye. I compare him to 'Abdul-'Uzza ibn Qatan. Any of you who survives to see him should recite over him the opening verses of soorat al-Kahf. He will appear on the way between Syria and Iraq and will spread mischief right and left. O servant of Allah! Adhere (to the path of truth). We said: Allah's Messenger, how long will he stay on the earth? He said: For forty days, one day like a year and one day like a month and one day like a week, and the rest of the days will be like your days. We said: Allah's Messenger, would one day's prayer suffice for the prayers of a day equal to one year? Thereupon he said: No, but you must make an estimate of time (and then observe prayer). We said: Allah's Messenger, how quickly will he walk upon the earth? He said: Like a cloud driven by the wind. He will come to the people and invite them (to a wrong religion), and they will affirm their faith in him and respond to him. He will then give a command to the sky; there will be rainfall upon the earth, and it will grow crops. Then in the evening, their pasturing animals will come to them with their humps very high,

their udders full of milk, and their flanks stretched. He will then come
to another people and invite them, but they will reject him. He will go
away from them; there will be drought for them, and nothing will be
left with them in the form of wealth. He will then walk through the
wasteland and say to it: Bring forth your treasures. The treasures will
come out and gather (themselves) before him like the swarm of bees.
He will then call a person brimming with youth, strike him with the
sword and cut him into two pieces, making these pieces lie at a
distance equivalent to that which is usually between the archer and his
target. He will then call that young man, and he will come forward
laughing, with his face gleaming (with happiness).» (Muslim)

Anas ibn Mâlik (رضي) reported that the Messenger of Allah
(ﷺ) said: «The Dajjâl will be followed by seventy thousand Jews of
Isfahan (a city in Iran) wearing Persian shawls.» (Muslim and at-
Tirmidhi)

According to other authentic hadiths, the Dajjâl will enter
every city on earth, with the exception of Makkah and Madinah.
«Narrated Abu Sa'eed al-Khudri: Allah's Apostle (ﷺ) told us a long
narrative about the Dajjâl, and among the many things he mentioned
was that the Dajjâl will come, and it will be forbidden for him to pass
through the entrances of Madinah. He will land in some of the salty
barren areas outside Madinah.» (Bukhari)

The Kharijites (terrorists) will fight alongside him, although
outwardly they seem to be pious Muslims.

«'Uqbah ibn 'Amr Abu Mas'ood al-Ansâri (رضي) reported: I
went to Hudhayfah ibn al-Yamân and said to him: Narrate what you
have heard from Allah's Messenger (ﷺ) pertaining to the Dajjâl. He
said that the Dajjâl will appear, and there will be water and fire with
him. What the people see as water will actually be fire, and it will
burn; what appears to be fire will be water. Any one of you who sees
that should plunge into that which you see as fire, for it will be sweet,

pure water. 'Uqbah said: I also heard it, confirming what Hudhayfah said.» (Muslim)

The Prophet (ﷺ) told us that firm, believing Muslims would go out to see him. Some will do so out of curiosity, while others will go out to debate with him. In the end, they will leave Islam and become believers in the Dajjâl, due to his persuasive speech and miraculous feats. He will even stand outside of Makkah and Madinah and call the people, and some people will leave Makkah and Madinah to see him. The Prophet (ﷺ) warned us not to give in to curiosity and go out and see him or to debate with him because we will not be able to defeat him; only Jesus (ﷺ) will.

Women will be especially vulnerable to the snares of the Dajjâl, because many women are naturally attracted to powerful men who can provide for them financially. If you have ever seen videos of the way many women in the modest 1950s culture reacted to Elvis Presley,[66] this will give you some idea. Throngs of women flocked to him; some would leave their families just to be near him. The Dajjâl will be extraordinarily attractive to women; according to a sound hadith recorded by Ahmad, they will make up the majority of his followers. In another sound narration recorded by Ahmad, the Prophet (ﷺ) said that men will have to tie down their wives and daughters to prevent them from going out to see the Dajjâl.[67]

---

[66] An American cultural icon, Elvis Presley was a musician known as 'the King of Rock and Roll'.

[67] This is not normally permissible for men to do to their wives. However, in our culture, we have a saying, "desperate times call for desperate measures." This will be a time that is more desperate than any other time in the history of the earth. In this time of desperation, this extreme measure will save those women from destruction.

The return of Jesus (⁑)

The Prophet (⁑) said: «Allah (⁑) will send Jesus (⁑), son of Mary, and he will descend at the white minaret in the eastern side of Damascus, wearing two garments lightly dyed with saffron, placing his hands on the wings of two angels. When he lowers his head, beads of perspiration will fall from his head, and when he raises it, beads like pearls will scatter from it. Every non-believer who smells his odour will die, and his breath will reach as far as he can see. He will then search for the Dajjâl until he catches hold of him at the gate of Ludd[68] and kills him.» (Muslim)

Jesus will break the cross, kill the pigs, and end every other religion on earth

The Prophet (⁑) said: «By him in whose hands my soul is, (Jesus) son of Mary will descend amongst you shortly as a just ruler and will break the cross,[69] kill the pig and abolish the *jizyah* (the tax paid by non-Muslims in lieu of zakâh). Wealth will flow so that nobody will accept it.» (Bukhari and Muslim)

The Prophet (⁑) said: «There is no prophet between me and him, that is, Jesus (⁑). He will descend (to the earth). When you see him, recognize him: a man of medium height, reddish fair, wearing two light yellow garments, looking as if drops were falling down from his head although it will not be wet. He will fight the people for the cause of Islam. He will break the cross, kill swine, and abolish jizyah. Allah (⁑) will make all religions perish except Islam. Jesus (⁑) will destroy the Antichrist. He will live on the earth for forty

---

[68] Ironically, this is now the site of Israel's Ben Gurion International Airport, which included an Israeli Air Force base for many years.

[69] This will end the divide between Christians and Muslims. They will return to the teachings of the scriptures and follow the truth.

years, and then he will die. The Muslims will pray over him.» (a sound hadith recorded by Abu Dâwood)

Sincere Jews and Christians will accept Jesus (ﷺ) as their Messiah, while the insincere ones will fight on the side of the Dajjâl. The Muslims will then kill all of the followers of the Dajjâl in battle.

'Abdullah ibn 'Amr ibn al-'Âs (ﷺ) reported that a person came to him and said: "What is this hadith that you narrate that the Last Hour would come at such and such time?" Thereupon he said: "Hallowed be Allah, there is no god but Allah (or words to that effect). I have decided that I will not narrate anything to anyone now. I had only said that you would see after some time an important event: that the (sacred) House (*Kaaba*) would be burnt, and it would definitely happen."

He then reported that Allah's Messenger (ﷺ) said: «The Dajjâl will appear in my Ummah, and he will stay (in the world) for forty. ['Abdullah ibn 'Amr ibn al-'Âs (ﷺ) could not say whether he meant for forty days, forty months or forty years.] Allah (ﷺ) will then send Jesus, son of Mary (ﷺ), who will resemble 'Urwa ibn Mas'ood. Jesus (ﷺ) will chase and kill the Dajjâl. After that, people will live for seven years, in which there will be no rancour between two persons. Then Allah (ﷺ) will send cold wind from the direction of Syria until no one who has a speck of good or faith in him will survive upon the earth. They will die, so much so that even if some amongst you were to enter the innermost part of the mountain, this wind would reach that place also, and cause your death.»

He heard Allah's Messenger (ﷺ) say: «Only the wicked people will survive, and they will be as careless as birds with the characteristics of beasts. They will never appreciate the good nor condemn the evil. Then Satan will come to them in human form and say: Do you not respond? They will say: What do you order us? He will command them to worship the idols but, in spite of this, they will have an abundance of sustenance and will lead comfortable lives. Then the trumpet will be blown, and everyone who hears that will bend his neck to one side and raise it from the other side. The first one to hear that trumpet will be the person who is busy in setting right the tank meant for providing water to the camels. He will swoon, and the other people will also swoon, then Allah (عَزَّوَجَلَّ) will send — or He will cause to send — rain, which will be like dew, and there will grow out of it the bodies of the people. Then the second trumpet will be blown, and they will stand up and begin to look (around). Then it will be said: O people, go to your Lord, and make them stand there, and they will be questioned.» (Muslim)

Abu Hurayrah (رَضِيَ اللهُ عَنْهُ) narrated that Allah's Apostle (صَلَّى اللهُ عَلَيْهِ وَسَلَّمَ) said: «By Him in Whose Hands my soul is, surely (Jesus) the son of Mary will soon descend amongst you and will judge mankind justly (as a just ruler); he will break the cross and kill the pigs, and there will be no jizyah. Money will be in abundance, so that nobody will accept it, and a single prostration to Allah (in prayer) will be better than the whole world and whatever is in it.» Abu Hurayrah (رَضِيَ اللهُ عَنْهُ) added: If you wish, you can recite: ﴿And there is none from the People of the Scripture but that he will surely believe in Jesus before his death. And on the Day of Resurrection he will be against them a witness.﴾ *(Qur'an 4: 159)* (Bukhari)

After Jesus (عَلَيْهِ السَّلَامُ)

«Hudhayfah ibn al-Yamân (رَضِيَ اللهُ عَنْهُ) said that the Prophet (صَلَّى اللهُ عَلَيْهِ وَسَلَّمَ) said: Islam will become worn out like clothes are, until there will be no one who knows what fasting, prayer, charity and rituals are. The Qur'an will disappear in one night, and no verse will be left on earth. Some groups of old people will be left who will say: We heard our fathers saying *lâ ilâha illâ Allâh* (there is none worthy of worship other than Allah), so we repeated it. Silah asked Ḥudhayfah: What will saying *lâ ilâha illâ Allâh* do for them when they do not know what prayer, fasting, ritual and charity are? Ḥudhayfah ignored him. Silah repeated his question three times, and each time Ḥudhayfah ignored him. Finally he answered: O Silah, it will save them from hell, and he said it three times.» (a sound hadith recorded by Ibn Mâjah)

The Prophet (ﷺ) said: «The Hour will not come upon anyone who says: Allah, Allah.» (Muslim)

He (ﷺ) also stated: «It will only come upon the most evil of people.» (Muslim)

He told us: «The sun will rise in the west instead of the east, and repentance will no longer be accepted.» (Bukhari and Muslim)

The Problem of Terrorism

$\mathcal{T}$he Prophet (ﷺ) predicted the coming of the Kharijites[70] (terrorists). Ibn 'Abbâs (﵁) narrated that the Prophet (ﷺ) said: «Among the offspring of this man will be some who will recite the Qur'an, but the Qur'an will not reach beyond their throats (in other words, they will recite like parrots without understanding it or acting on it), and they will renegade from the religion as an arrow goes through the prey's body. They will kill the Muslims but will not disturb the idolaters. If I am living at their time, I will kill them as the people of 'Âd were killed (meaning: I will kill all of them).» (Bukhari)

These groups and their followers are Kharijites despite being very outwardly religious in many cases [and this is exactly as the Prophet (ﷺ) told us they would be]. What takes the Kharijites outside the teachings of Islam is that they reject the Sunnah and the Sharia in regards to the sanctity of blood and the rulings of military combat. Before we go into this, we must discuss the types of physical *jihad* (armed combat) and the roles and rights of the Muslim governments (whether pious or corrupt).

Jihad (struggle or striving in the cause of Allah) is one of the most controversial topics in the world right now. The terrorist groups and the neoconservative Christians go to one extreme, redefining what the Sharia has to say about jihad and teaching that Islam is a religion of perpetual warfare. The apologetic Muslims and the

---

[70] 'Kharijites' is an English term based on the Arabic word *Khawârij*, meaning 'those who go out or leave (the true teachings of Islam)'. For detailed proof of who the Kharijites are, along with a description of actions perpetrated by Muslims today who are considered Kharijites, see Aali-'Ubaykaan, *The Khawaarij and their Recurring Methodologies*.

Western liberals go to the other extreme, defining jihad as merely a struggle against the evil of one's nafs and defining Islam as a religion that only advocates peace. Both sides use verses of the Qur'an, as well as quotes from classical and modern scholars of Islam, to back up their arguments — but both are incorrect. The reality is in between the two extremes.

Islam gives us guidance in all aspects of life: religious, political, social and economic. From the ages of forty to fifty-three, the Prophet Muhammad (ﷺ) was a religious leader; from the ages of fifty-three until his death at sixty-three, he (ﷺ) was also the leader of a government.

As political leaders, the Prophet (ﷺ) and his successors (may Allah be pleased with them) dealt with four groups of people:

1. Muslims (who paid zakâh)
2. Non-Muslims under the protection of the Muslim government (who paid the jizyah tax in lieu of zakâh)
3. Non-Muslim nations who fulfilled the agreements in their treaties
4. Non-Muslim nations who were at war with the Muslim nation, or who indicated that war was likely

His successor Abu Bakr (ﷺ), the first caliph, had to deal with a fifth group: Muslims who refused to pay zakâh. The third and fourth caliphs, 'Uthmân ibn 'Affân and 'Ali ibn Abu Ṭâlib (may Allah be pleased with the Rightly-guided first four caliphs) had to deal with a sixth group: revolutionaries or insurrectionists.

It is illegal to kill any of the people in the first two categories unless they have committed a crime where the punishment is the death penalty — and then only after they have been put to trial and found guilty.

It is illegal to attack those in the third category. For example, in the 'golden age of Islam', Muslims made treaties with China and

Ethiopia, and neither side attacked the other. Muslims were allowed to travel to those countries for trade, to invite people in those countries to Islam, and to establish communities within those countries. Likewise, the Chinese and Ethiopians sent people to Muslim countries to trade.

The only permissible physical jihad is with those in the fourth, fifth and sixth categories. There are two types of physical jihad: defensive and offensive. Defensive jihad occurs when another nation is trying to take over land or homes; in this case, it is obligatory on every male to fight to protect what is his. Offensive jihad is an offensive war that occurs because of a legitimate threat to a Muslim nation. It requires an official declaration of jihad made by the Muslim ruler of that nation (whether he is a caliph, king, dictator, president or prime minister).

When undertaking a jihad, there are rules to be followed. The intention must be to fight for Allah (ﷻ), and the soldiers must follow the laws of combat sent down by Allah (ﷻ) and explained by the Prophet Muhammad (ﷺ) in authentic hadiths. It is forbidden (according to the authentic teachings of the Prophet Muhammad) to kill women, children, monks, priests, nuns, and rabbis — unless they are soldiers or combatants. In the past, some non-Muslims knew that and used their women and children as human shields to compel Muslim armies to retreat from battle.

A Muslim soldier follows these rules of combat. On the other hand, Kharijites follow the laws of Satan, the laws of the jungle, the laws of Karl Marx[71] and John Locke[72], and other innovated methodologies, in the name of Islam.

---

[71] A nineteenth century German philosopher who was one of the founders of modern communism [Editor]

[72] A seventeenth century Englishman known as the 'father of liberalism' [Editor]

The Kharijites kill many Muslims and non-combatants. The bombing of the Australian embassy in Indonesia, in September 2004, resulted in the deaths of Muslim employees and visitors. Many Muslims and non-Muslim civilians who worked at New York's World Trade Center were killed on September 11, 2001. The suicide attacks seen in Iraq in recent years have killed many Muslims.

The Kharijites also consider it permissible to assassinate rulers of Muslim countries and to overthrow their governments, despite the fact that there are numerous hadiths (some of which were mentioned previously) where the Prophet (ﷺ) clearly and unequivocally forbade this. They also consider it permissible to kill any Muslim who is against their plots to overthrow governments or who supports leaving the rulers in power.

The Kharijites also follow rogue leaders who have no state authority, and they allow these leaders to declare jihad. The true Muslim recognizes that jihad is only lawful when it is declared by a legitimate ruler or head of state.

The Kharijites consider suicide bombing to be permissible, despite all of the evidence from clear and unequivocal hadiths that it is not allowed.

The Prophet (ﷺ) said: «Whoever purposely throws himself from a mountain and kills himself, he will be in the hellfire falling down into it and abiding therein perpetually forever; whoever drinks poison and kills himself with it, he will be carrying his poison in his hand and drinking it in the hellfire wherein he will abide eternally forever; and whoever kills himself with an iron weapon, he will be carrying that weapon in his hand and stabbing his abdomen with it in the hellfire wherein he will abide eternally forever.» (Bukhari)

Abu Hurayrah (ﺭﺿﻲ) narrated that Allah's Messenger (ﷺ) said: «None amongst you should make a request for death, and do not call for it before it comes, for when any of you dies, he ceases (to do good) deeds. The life of a believer is not prolonged but for goodness.» (Muslim)

Anas ibn Mâlik (🙏) reported Allah's Messenger (🙏) as saying: «None of you should make a request for death because of the trouble in which he is involved, but if there is no other help for it, then say: O Allah, keep me alive as long as there is goodness in life for me, and bring death to me when there is goodness in death for me.» (Muslim)

Abu Hurayrah (🙏) narrated that Allah's Messenger (🙏) said: «Do not wish for death nor pray for it, lest it come to you. Indeed, when (a person) dies, his hopes are cut off; and a Muslim's age only increases good for him.» (Muslim)

Abu Hurayrah (🙏) narrated that Allah's Messenger (🙏) said: «Do not wish for death; if one is a doer of good, it may be that his good deeds will increase, and if he is a wrongdoer, it may be that he will (truly) repent.» (Bukhari)

The Prophet (🙏) said: «There was amongst those before you a man who had a wound. He was in such anguish that he took a knife and used it to make a cut in his hand, and the blood did not stop flowing until he died. Allah the Almighty said: My servant has himself forestalled Me; I have forbidden him paradise.» (Bukhari and Muslim)

«Narrated Sahl ibn Sa'd as-Sa'idi (🙏): Allah's Apostle (🙏) and the pagans faced each other and started fighting. When Allah's Apostle (🙏) returned to his camp and the pagans returned to their camp, somebody talked about a man amongst the Companions of Allah's Apostle (🙏) who would follow and kill with his sword any pagan going alone. He said: Nobody did his job (of fighting) as properly today as that man. Allah's Apostle (🙏) said: Indeed, he is amongst the people of the hellfire. A man amongst the people said: I shall accompany him (to watch what he does). Thus he accompanied him; wherever he stood, he would stand with him, and wherever he ran, he would run with him. Then the (brave) man became seriously wounded, so he decided to bring about his death quickly. He planted the blade of the sword in the ground, directing its sharp end towards his chest between his two breasts. Then he leaned on the sword and killed himself.

The other man came to Allah's Apostle (ﷺ) and said: I testify that you are the Apostle of Allah. The Prophet (ﷺ) asked: What has happened?

He replied: (It is about) the man whom you had described as one of the people of the hellfire. The people were greatly surprised at what you said, and I said: I will find out his reality for you. So I came out seeking him. He got severely wounded and hastened to die by slanting the blade of his sword in the ground, directing its sharp end towards his chest between his two breasts. Then he eased on his sword and killed himself.

Allah's Apostle (ﷺ) said: A man may seem to the people as if he were practicing the deeds of the people of paradise, while in fact he is from the people of the hellfire. Another may seem to the people as if he were practicing the deeds of the people of hellfire, while in fact he is from the people of paradise.» (Bukhari)

❲...And do not kill yourselves [or one another]. Indeed, Allah is to you ever Merciful.❳ *(Qur'an 4: 29)*

«The Prophet (ﷺ) said that Allah (ﷻ) said: I will declare war against one who shows hostility to a pious worshipper of Mine. The most beloved things with which My slave comes nearer to Me are what I have enjoined upon him, and My slave keeps on coming closer to Me through performing extra deeds (besides what is obligatory) until I love him. I become his sense of hearing with which he hears, his sense of sight with which he sees, his hand with which he grips, and his leg with which he walks. If he asks Me, I will give him, and if he asks My protection, I will protect him. I do not hesitate to do anything as I hesitate to take the soul of the believer, for he hates death, and I hate to disappoint him.» (Bukhari)

The Kharijite scholars can read all of these clear proofs from the Qur'an and Sunnah and still say that suicide bombing is permissible if one has nothing else to fight with. The Prophet Muhammad (ﷺ) did not make this exception in these hadiths. The Kharijites are like the Christians, who made their priests and monks into gods by allowing them to say that something was permissible even when their own scriptures said that it was forbidden. It is one of the signs of the end of time that people (scholars included) will declare permissible things that Allah (ﷻ) has declared forbidden. This is why Allah (ﷻ) warned us in the Qur'an not to follow anyone blindly. This is why jurists produce evidence for their rulings. You might blindly follow someone who is teaching you something that goes against what the Prophet (ﷺ) taught and, despite your sincere intention, you might cause great harm to people.[73]

This applies to all scholars, past and present. Even fountains of knowledge, such as Imam Mâlik ibn Anas (may Allah have mercy on him), taught that they should not be followed blindly.[74] Those who

---

[73] Every action has two parts to be acceptable to Allah (ﷻ): first, one must have a sincere intention to do it solely seeking the pleasure of Allah; second, the action must be done the way the Prophet (ﷺ) did it and not in opposition to the way that he did it.

[74] I am not advocating abandoning *madh-habs* (schools of Islamic law). The Sunnah of the Prophet (ﷺ) was preserved through madh-habs. However, if you are convinced that the evidence of another scholar is stronger than the position of your madh-hab, you have to follow the evidence, because true scholars are trying to follow the Sunnah of the Prophet (ﷺ). The goal is to reach Allah (ﷻ) by following the Prophet (ﷺ), and every scholar makes=

promote blind following claim that anyone who believes that *ijtihâd* (independently deriving legal rulings from the Qur'an and Sunnah) is still a valid method in our times is ignorant and even arrogant. Yet the people who promote blind following do not go into the details of their own rulings or provide evidence for them.

For example, Imam Mâlik stated that if a married (or previously married) woman is pregnant and claims that she has been raped, but she cannot prove it by signs of struggle (such as torn clothing or marks on the body), then she is to be executed for adultery.[75] Imam Mâlik was one of the greatest scholars of the Ummah, and we are indebted to him; however, if we follow him blindly in this case, we will cause great harm and injustice on the earth. Imam Mâlik made this ruling based on the knowledge that he had, but he did not have the knowledge that we have today about the 'fight, flight, or freeze' response. When people are in extremely stressful situations, they either fight, run away from the situation, or totally panic and freeze. The majority of rape victims go into a state of shock and freeze, like a deer in headlights. If Imam Mâlik had that knowledge, I do not think that he would have made that legal ruling. Other imams gave the correct legal ruling, which is that if the woman says she was raped, we accept her testimony, and she is not punished for adultery.

By blindly following someone, even one of the Ummah's greatest scholars, Muslim governments could end up executing thousands of innocent women and causing oppression on the earth. If the great Imam Mâlik were alive today, and he had knowledge of the human body's 'fight, flight, or freeze' response to stress, I believe

---

=mistakes. We all have to stand alone before Allah (ﷻ) on the Day of Judgment, so we have to seek the truth and follow it.

[75] Ibn Rushd, *The Distinguished Jurist's Primer*, Vol. 2

that he would change his ruling. He was a person who would submit to convincing evidence, as he did when Imam Shâfiʻi (may Allah have mercy on him) brought him evidence that was contrary to one of his previous judgments. True followers of any Islamic school of law, or of any scholar, will set aside the statement of that scholar when there is authentic, stronger textual evidence that supports another legal ruling. When you truly follow someone, you do what he or she would have done in the same situation.

If the people do not have the weapons to fight with, then they should make themselves stronger by following the Sunnah and the Sharia. When the Prophet (ﷺ) was in Makkah, he was not the head of state, and he only had about seventy followers. He did not attempt an insurrection or suggest suicide missions. In fact, when he saw his followers being persecuted and asking for help, he told them to be patient. He taught his followers that if they continued practicing tawḥeed, worshipping Allah (ﷻ) alone, following the Sunnah of the Prophet (ﷺ) and purifying their hearts, then Allah (ﷻ) would grant them power on the earth, and they would conquer the superpowers that surrounded them: Persia and Rome. As crazy as that seemed, they listened to him, and within thirty years, that small band of mostly weak and persecuted followers had become the dominant military, religious, political, and economic power on the earth. They crushed the Persian and Byzantine empires, which the Arabs had believed were unbeatable; as a result, many of the oppressed subjects of the Persian and Byzantine empires rushed to embrace Islam.

The Prophet (ﷺ) even told us what to do if the Muslims have no ruler, according to this report from Ḥudhayfah (ؓ): «When people were asking the Prophet Muhammad (ﷺ) about the goodness, I was asking about the evil, in fear that it might get to me. I asked: O Prophet of Allah (ﷺ), we were in jâhiliyah, then Allah brought this goodness; will there be any evil after it? The Prophet Muhammad

(ﷺ) said: Yes, there will. I said: Will there be goodness after it? He (ﷺ) said: Yes, but it will have some impurities. I asked: And what are its impurities? He (ﷺ) said: Some people will guide others not according to my tradition. You will approve of some of their deeds and disapprove of some others. I asked: Is there evil after this goodness? He (ﷺ) said: Yes, there will be preachers calling at the gates of hellfire; whoever responds to their call will be thrown by them into the hellfire. So I said: O Prophet of Allah (ﷺ), describe them for us. He (ﷺ) said: They are from you, and they speak our language. So I asked: What should I do if I witness that? The Prophet (ﷺ) said: Stick with the group of Muslims and their leader. I asked: What if they have no leader? He (ﷺ) said: If they have no leader or imam, then leave all these groups, even if you have to bite on a tree until you meet Allah (ﷻ) while you are still in that state.» (Bukhari)

Therefore, they need to follow the Sunnah and the Sharia one hundred percent, and Allah (ﷻ) will eventually make a way out for them and all of us. The Sunnah might be hard at first, but it is the path to happiness and success in this life and the next. Acting impatiently, and using innovated methods such as revolutions and suicide bombs, has hurt Muslims and non-Muslims physically and spiritually all over the world and has brought about no good. Remember that according to the Qur'an, Allah (ﷻ) will not change our condition until we change what is inside ourselves, and He (ﷻ) will not rectify our condition until we purify our hearts of the diseases mentioned earlier.

❴Indeed, Allah will not change the condition of a people until they change what is in themselves.❵ *(Qur'an 13: 11)*

The Kharijites also use the argument that the non-Muslims terrorize the Muslim nations and kill civilians, women and children, so the Muslims should do the same. However, the proof that Islam is true is the moral superiority of practicing Muslims over the rest of the peoples of the world. Of course, there are good Muslims and bad

Muslims, just as there are nice non-Muslims and horrible non-Muslims. However, anyone who spends a considerable period of time with practicing Muslims realizes that practicing Muslims are by far morally and religiously superior to non-Muslims. This is why most of the people who are around practicing Muslims for an extended period of time end up becoming Muslim or hating (and even sometimes trying to kill) Muslims.

Our standards of 'good' are totally different. For example, who is a good baseball player? Children on a little league baseball team might pick any John Doe for their traveling all-star team. A major leaguer, on the other hand, might choose Alex Rodriguez (A-Rod).[76] In reality, there is no comparison between A-Rod and John Doe; John Doe would look awful in the highest levels of professional baseball, despite the fact that he looks good next to children in the youth leagues. Practicing Muslims are like A-Rod, and non-Muslims are like John Doe. That is the reason why many non-Muslims become so cynical (and think poorly of people) in old age, and many Muslims do not. We have higher standards of goodness, so we produce better results. Only four Muslim missionaries went to Indonesia, and now there are over 200 million Muslims in Indonesia.[77] They saw superior human beings and wanted to be like them. However, if Muslims use the disbelieving politicians as our standard of behaviour, then we might scare 200 million people away from Islam.

---

[76] Alex Rodriguez, nicknamed 'A-Rod', is considered to be one of the best all-around baseball players in the U.S. at the time of this writing. [Editor]

[77] 2009 estimate, taken from CIA World Fact Book [Editor]

Seeking Help with Life's Decisions

When you have a problem in life, or a decision to make, you should ask Allah (ﷺ) to guide you in making that decision and show you the right course.

Supplication for seeking guidance in forming a decision or choosing the proper course (istikhârah)

اللَّهُمَّ إِنِّي أَسْتَخِيرُكَ بِعِلْمِكَ، وَأَسْتَقْدِرُكَ بِقُدْرَتِكَ، وَأَسْأَلُكَ مِنْ فَضْلِكَ الْعَظِيمِ، فَإِنَّكَ تَقْدِرُ وَلاَ أَقْدِرُ، وَتَعْلَمُ، وَلاَ أَعْلَمُ، وَأَنْتَ عَلَّامُ الْغُيُوبِ، اللَّهُمَّ إِنْ كُنْتَ تَعْلَمُ أَنَّ هَذَا الْأَمْرَ- خَيْرٌ لِي فِي دِينِي وَمَعَاشِي وَعَاقِبَةِ أَمْرِي- عَاجِلِهِ وَآجِلِهِ- فَاقْدُرْهُ لِي وَيَسِّرْهُ لِي ثُمَّ بَارِكْ لِي فِيهِ، وَإِنْ كُنْتَ تَعْلَمُ أَنَّ هَذَا الْأَمْرَ شَرٌّ لِي فِي دِينِي وَمَعَاشِي وَعَاقِبَةِ أَمْرِي- عَاجِلِهِ وَآجِلِهِ- فَاصْرِفْهُ عَنِّي وَاصْرِفْنِي عَنْهُ وَاقْدُرْ لِيَ الْخَيْرَ حَيْثُ كَانَ ثُمَّ أَرْضِنِي بِهِ

«On the authority of Jâbir ibn 'Abdullah (ﷺ): The Prophet (ﷺ) would instruct us to pray for guidance in all of our concerns, just as he would teach us a chapter from the Qur'an. He (ﷺ) would say: If any of you intends to undertake a matter, then let him pray two units of optional prayer, after which he should supplicate: *Allâhumma innee astakheeruka bi-'ilmika, wa astaqdiruka bi-qudratika, wa as'aluka min faḍlika al-'adheem, fa innaka taqdiru wa lâ aqdiru, wa ta'lamu, wa lâ a'lamu, wa anta 'allâmu al-ghuyoob. Allâhumma in kunta ta'lamu hâdha al-amr [then mention the thing to be decided] khayrun lee fee deenee wa ma'âshee wa 'âqibati amree faqdirhu lee wa yassirhu lee thumma bârik lee feehi, wa in kunta ta'lamu anna hâdhal-amra sharrun lee fee deenee wa ma'âshee wa 'âqibati amree faṣrifhu 'annee waṣrifnee 'anhu waqdir leeyal-khayra haythu kâna thumma ardinee bih.* [O Allah! I consult You in Your knowledge, and appeal to You to strengthen me by Your Omnipotence and beseech Your great favour, and You certainly know best while I do not know, and can do everything while I cannot. You are the Knower of the unseen. O Allah, if You know that this affair (then mention the thing to be decided) is good for me, my religion, my life on this earth and in the hereafter, then let (the thing I choose) be for me. But if you know that this affair is bad for my religion, my life on this earth and in the hereafter, then keep it away from me, and keep me away from it. And choose good for me wherever it is, and let me be content with it.]» (Bukhari)

Virtuous Actions that Can Prevent Problems from Occurring

$\mathcal{J}$f you were to examine most of the problems that you caused in your life, you would have to admit that if had been doing something better with your time, you would not have been in that situation. The Prophet (ﷺ) encouraged us by teaching us many beneficial ways to spend our time, ways that can prevent us from experiencing these difficulties. Listed below are a variety of the Prophet's statements suggesting things that we can do with our time that will benefit us and keep problems away from us.

Types of charity

The Prophet (ﷺ) said: «Every act of goodness is charity.» (Muslim)

«The Prophet Muhammad (ﷺ) said: Every Muslim has to give in charity. The people then asked: (What) if someone has nothing to give, what should he do? The Prophet (ﷺ) replied: He should work with his hands and benefit himself and also give in charity (from what he earns). The people further asked: If he cannot find even that? He replied: He should help the needy who appeal for help. Then the people asked: If he cannot do (even) that? The Prophet said finally: Then he should perform good deeds and keep away from evil deeds, and that will be regarded as carrying out charitable deeds.» (Bukhari)

The Prophet Muhammad (ﷺ) said: «Charity is due on every joint of a person, every day the sun rises. Administering justice between two men is also a charity; assisting a man to ride upon his beast, or helping him load his luggage upon it, is a charity; a good word is a charity; every step that you take towards prayer is a charity;

and removing harmful things from the pathway is a charity.» (Bukhari and Muslim)

He also said: «Your smile for your brother is charity.» (a sound hadith recorded by at-Tirmidhi)

The Prophet Muhammad (ﷺ) said: «Save yourself from hellfire by giving even half a date (fruit) in charity.» (Bukhari)

❲They ask you, [O Muhammad], what they should spend. Say: Whatever you spend of good is [to be] for parents and relatives and orphans and the needy and the traveler. And whatever you do of good — indeed, Allah is Knowing of it.❳ *(Qur'an 2: 215)*

Abu Mas'ood al-Badri narrated that the Messenger of Allah (ﷺ) said: «When a man spends to support his family, hoping (for the reward from Allah), it is counted for him as charity.» (Bukhari and Muslim)

It has been narrated on the authority of Abu Hurayrah (ﷺ) that he heard the Messenger of Allah (ﷺ) say: «The believers who show the most perfect faith are those who have the best character, and the best of you are those who are best to their wives.» (a sound hadith recorded by at-Tirmidhi)

Visiting the sick

«Allah (ﷺ) said: O son of Adam, I fell ill and you did not visit Me. He will say: O Lord, and how should I visit You when You are the Lord of the worlds? He (ﷺ) will say: Did you not know that My servant so-and-so had fallen ill, and you did not visit him? Did you not know that had you visited him, you would have found Me with him? O son of Adam, I asked you for food and you did not feed Me. He will say: O Lord, and how should I feed You when You are the Lord of the worlds? He will say: Did you not know that My servant so-and-so asked you for food and you did not feed him? Did you not know that had you fed him, you would surely have found that (the reward for doing so) with Me? O son of Adam, I asked you to give Me to drink and you did not give Me to drink. He will say: O Lord, how should I give You to drink when You are the Lord of the worlds? He will say: My servant so-and-so asked you to give him to drink, and you did not give him to drink. Had you given him to drink, you would have surely found that with Me.» (Muslim)

Greeting one another

'Abdullah ibn Salâm (رضي) reported that he heard the Messenger of Allah (ﷺ) say: «O people, exchange greetings of peace (by saying *as-salâmu 'alaykum* to one another), feed people, strengthen the ties of kinship, and be in prayer when others are asleep; you will enter paradise in peace.» (a sound hadith recorded by at-Tirmidhi)

Abu Hurayrah (رضي) reported that the Messenger of Allah (ﷺ) said: «By Him in Whose Hand is my life! You will not enter paradise until you believe, and you will not believe until you love one another. Shall I inform you of something by which, if you do it, you will love one another? Promote greetings amongst yourselves (by saying *as-salâmu 'alaykum*).» (Muslim)

«'Abdullah ibn 'Amr ibn al-'Âs (رضي) reported that a man asked the Messenger of Allah (ﷺ): Which act in Islam is the best? He (ﷺ) replied: To give food and to greet everyone, whether you know them or not.» (Bukhari and Muslim)

Brotherhood and sisterhood

Abu Hurayrah (رضي) reported that the Messenger of Allah (ﷺ) said: «Do not be envious of one another, do not artificially inflate prices against one another, do not hate one another, do not shun one another, do not undercut one another in business transactions, and be as fellow-brothers and servants of Allah (ﷻ).» (Muslim)

Abu Hurayrah (ﷺ) narrated that the Prophet (ﷺ) said: «Whoever relieves a believer of some grief pertaining to this world, Allah (ﷻ) will relieve him of some grief pertaining to the hereafter. Whoever alleviates the difficulties of a needy person who cannot pay his debt, Allah (ﷻ) will alleviate his difficulties in both this world and the hereafter. Whoever conceals the faults of a Muslim, Allah (ﷻ) will conceal his faults in this world and the hereafter. Allah (ﷻ) will aid a servant (of His) as long as the servant aids his brother. Whoever follows a path to seek knowledge therein, Allah will make easy for him a path to paradise. No people gather together in one of the houses of Allah, reciting the Book of Allah and studying it among themselves, except that tranquility descends upon them, mercy covers them, the angels surround them, and Allah makes mention of them among those who are in His presence. Whoever is slowed down by his deeds will not be hastened forward by his lineage.» (Muslim)

Virtues of reading and reciting the Qur'an

Abu Umamah (ﷺ) reported that he heard the Messenger of Allah (ﷺ) say: «Read the Qur'an, for it will come as an intercessor for its reciters on the Day of Resurrection.» (Muslim)

'Uthmân ibn 'Affân (ﷺ) reported that the Messenger of Allah (ﷺ) said: «The best among you is the one who learns the Qur'an and teaches it.» (Bukhari)

'Â'ishah (ﷺ) reported that the Messenger of Allah (ﷺ) said: «The one who is proficient in the recitation of the Qur'an will be with the honourable and obedient scribes (angels). He who recites the Qur'an and finds it difficult to recite, doing his best to recite it in the best way possible, will have a double reward.» (Bukhari and Muslim)

Abu Moosâ al-Ash'ari (ﷺ) reported that the Messenger of Allah (ﷺ) said: «The believer who recites the Qur'an is like a citron, whose fragrance is sweet and whose taste is delicious. A believer who does not recite the Qur'an is like a date (fruit), which has no fragrance but has a sweet taste. The hypocrite who recites the Qur'an is like a colocynth (bitter apple), whose fragrance is so sweet, but its taste is bitter. The hypocrite who does not recite the Qur'an is like basil, which has no fragrance, and its taste is bitter.» (Bukhari and Muslim)

Ibn Mas'ood (ﷺ) reported that the Messenger of Allah (ﷺ) said: «Whoever recites a letter from the Book of Allah, he will be credited with a good deed, and a good deed gets a ten-fold reward. I do not say that *alif-lâm-meem* is one letter, but *alif* is a letter, *lâm* is a letter and *meem* is a letter.» (Muslim)

Abu Hurayrah (ﷺ) narrated that the Messenger of Allah (ﷺ) said: «Do not turn your homes into graves. Certainly, Satan runs away from a house in which soorat al-Baqarah is recited.» (Muslim)

«Abu Sa'eed al-Khudri (ﷺ) reported: A man heard another man reciting soorat al-Ikhlâṣ repeatedly. The next morning, he came to the Messenger of Allah (ﷺ) and informed him about it, as if he considered it to be of little reward. The Messenger of Allah (ﷺ) said: By Him in Whose Hand my soul is, this chapter is equal to one-third of the Qur'an.» (Bukhari)

Abu Hurayrah (ﷺ) reported that he heard the Messenger of Allah (ﷺ) say: «There is a chapter in the Qur'an that contains thirty verses that keep interceding for a person until his sins are forgiven. This chapter is 'Blessed is He in Whose Hand is the dominion' (soorat al-Mulk).» (a reliable hadith recorded by at-Tirmidhi and Abu Dâwood)

Abu Mas'ood al-Badri (ﷺ) reported that he heard the Prophet (ﷺ) say: «He who recites the two verses at the end of soorat al-Baqarah at night, they will suffice him.» (Bukhari and Muslim)

Virtues of ablution

«Abu Hurayrah (ﷺ) reported: I heard my beloved friend and companion (ﷺ) saying: The adornment of the believer (in paradise) will reach the places where the water of ablution reaches (his body).» (Muslim)

'Uthmân ibn Affân (ﷺ) reported that the Messenger of Allah (ﷺ) said: «He who performs the ablution perfectly, his sins will depart from his body, even from under his nails.» (Muslim)

Abu Hurayrah (ﷺ) reported that the Messenger of Allah (ﷺ) said: «When a Muslim, or a believer, washes his face (in the course of making ablution), every sin which he committed with his eyes will be washed away from his face with water, or with the last drop of water; when he washes his hands, every sin that was committed by his hands will be erased from his hands with the water, or with the last drop of water; and when he washes his feet, every sin his feet committed will be washed away with the water, or with the last drop of water, until he finally emerges cleansed of all his sins.» (Muslim)

«Abu Hurayrah (ﷺ) reported that the Messenger of Allah (ﷺ) said: Shall I not tell you something by which Allah (ﷺ) effaces the sins and elevates ranks (in paradise)? The Companions said: Certainly, O Messenger of Allah. He (ﷺ) said: Performing the ablutions thoroughly in spite of difficult circumstances, walking with more paces to the mosque, and waiting for the next prayer after observing a prayer.» (Muslim)

Virtues of congregational prayer and Friday prayer

Abu Hurayrah (رضي الله عنه) reported that the Messenger of Allah (ﷺ) said: «The five (daily) prayers and the Friday prayer to the Friday prayer expiate whatever (minor sins) may be committed in between, as long as major sins are avoided.» (Muslim)

Abu Hurayrah (رضي الله عنه) reported that the Messenger of Allah (ﷺ) said: «Were people to know the blessing of pronouncing the call to prayer and standing in the first row, they would even draw lots to secure these privileges. Were they to realize the reward of performing prayer early, they would race for it. Were they to know the merits of the prayer after nightfall and the dawn prayer, they would come to them even if they had to crawl.» (Bukhari and Muslim)

«Abu Hurayrah (رضي الله عنه) reported that he heard the Messenger of Allah (ﷺ) say: If there were a river at the door of one of you, in which he takes a bath five times a day, would any dirt remain on him? They replied: No dirt would be left on him. He (ﷺ) said: That is the five obligatory prayers. Allah (عز وجل) obliterates all sins as a result of performing them.» (Bukhari and Muslim)

Abu Hurayrah (رضي الله عنه) reported that the Prophet (ﷺ) said: «He who purifies himself (performs ablutions) in his house and then walks to one of the houses of Allah (عز وجل) to perform an obligatory prayer, one step of his will wipe out his sins, and another step will elevate his rank (in paradise).» (Muslim)

«Ubayy ibn Ka'b (رضي الله عنه) reported: There was a man of the Anṣâr whose house was the farthest from the mosque. As far as I know, he never missed a prayer (in congregation). It was said to him: If you buy a donkey, you may ride upon it in the dark nights and on the hot days. He said: I do not want my house to be situated close to the mosque. I desire that my walking towards the mosque and returning home be recorded to my credit. Upon hearing this, the Messenger of Allah (ﷺ) said: Allah has gathered all (rewards) for you.» (Muslim)

Abu Moosâ al-Ash'ari (﵁) reported that the Messenger of Allah (ﷺ) said: «The person who will receive the highest reward for prayer is the one who comes to perform it in the mosque from the farthest distance, and he who waits for the prayer to perform it with the imam (in congregation) will have a greater reward than the one who observes it alone and then goes to sleep.» (Bukhari and Muslim)

Ibn 'Umar (﵁) reported that the Messenger of Allah (ﷺ) said: «Prayer in congregation is twenty-seven times more meritorious than prayer performed individually.» (Bukhari and Muslim)

'Abdullah ibn Mas'ood (﵁) reported: "He who wants to meet Allah (ﷺ) tomorrow as a Muslim should take care and observe the prayers when the call to prayer is announced for them. Allah (ﷺ) has explained to your Prophet (ﷺ) the ways of right guidance, and these (the prayers) are part of the right guidance. If you have to perform prayer in your houses, as this man who stays away and performs prayer in his house, you will abandon the Sunnah of your Prophet (ﷺ), and departing from the Sunnah of your Prophet (ﷺ) will lead you astray. No man purifies himself, doing it well, then approaches one of those mosques without Allah recording a blessing for him for every step he takes, raising him a degree for it and erasing a sin from him for it. I have seen the time when no one stayed behind except a well-known hypocrite. I also saw that a man was brought swaying (on account of weakness) between two men until he was set up in a (prayer) row." (Muslim)

'Uthmân ibn 'Affân (﵁) reported that he heard the Messenger of Allah (ﷺ) saying: «If one performs the nightfall prayer in congregation, it is as if he has performed prayer for half of the night. If one performs the dawn prayer in congregation, it is as if he has performed prayer the whole night.» (Muslim)

'Â'ishah (ﷺ) reported that the Prophet (ﷺ) said: «The two units of prayer before the dawn prayer are better than this world and all it contains.» (Muslim)

Abu Hurayrah (ﷺ) reported that the Messenger of Allah (ﷺ) said: «If anyone performs ablutions properly, then comes to the Friday prayer, listens to the sermon attentively and keeps silent, his (minor) sins between that Friday and the following Friday will be forgiven, with the addition of three more days....» (Muslim)

Abu Hurayrah (ﷺ) reported that the Prophet (ﷺ) said: «The five daily prayers, and from the Friday (prayer) to the next Friday (prayer), and the fasting of Ramadan to the next Ramadan, are expiation of the sins committed in between them, so long as major sins are avoided.» (Muslim)

Salmân al-Fârsi (ﷺ) reported that the Messenger of Allah (ﷺ) said: «If a man takes a bath on Friday, (or) purifies himself as much as he can with ablutions, oils his hair, applies whatever perfume is available in his house, sets forth for the mosque, does not separate two people (to make a seat for himself), performs the prayer that is prescribed for him, and remains silent when the imam speaks, his (minor) sins between that Friday and the following Friday will be forgiven.» (Bukhari)

Virtues of Ramadan and other times

Abu Hurayrah (ﷺ) reported that the Messenger of Allah (ﷺ) said: «He who observes optional night prayers throughout Ramadan, out of sincerity of faith and in the hope of earning a reward, will have his past sins pardoned. (Bukhari and Muslim)

Abu Hurayrah (ﷺ) reported that the Prophet (ﷺ) said: «He who observes fasting during the month of Ramadan with faith, while seeking its reward from Allah, will have his past sins forgiven.» (Bukhari and Muslim)

«Ibn 'Abbâs (◌) reported: The Messenger of Allah (◌) was the most generous of men, and he was the most generous during the month of Ramadan, when Jibreel (◌) visited him every night and recited the Qur'an to him. During this period, the generosity of the Messenger of Allah (◌) expanded more quickly than the rain bearing wind.» (Bukhari and Muslim)

«'Â'ishah (◌) reported: When the last ten nights (of Ramadan) would begin, the Messenger of Allah (◌) would stay awake at night (for prayer and devotion), awaken his family and prepare himself to be more diligent in worship.» (Bukhari and Muslim)

Abu Hurayrah (◌) reported that the Messenger of Allah (◌) said: «The best month for observing fasting, after Ramadan, is the month of Allah (◌), Muḥarram; the best prayer after the prescribed prayers is prayer at night (the voluntary late night prayer).» (Muslim)

«Ibn 'Abbâs (◌) reported that the Messenger of Allah (◌) said: There are no days during which a righteous action is more pleasing to Allah than these days (the first ten days of the Islamic month of Dhul-Ḥijjah). He was asked: O Messenger of Allah, not even jihad in the cause of Allah (◌)? He (◌) replied: Not even jihad in the cause of Allah, except in the case when one goes forth with his life and his property and does not return with either of them.» (Bukhari)

«Abu Qatâdah (◌) reported that the Messenger of Allah (◌) was asked about the observance of fasting on the day of 'Arafât (during the hajj). He said: It is an expiation for the sins of the preceding year and the current year.» (Muslim)

Abu Ayyoob al-Anṣâri (◌) reported that the Messenger of Allah (◌) said: «If one observed the fast of Ramadan, and then followed it by fasting six days in the month of Shawwal, it is as if he fasted for the whole year.» (Muslim)

«Abu Qatâdah (ﷺ) reported that the Messenger of Allah (ﷺ) was asked about fasting on Mondays. He said: That is the day on which I was born and the day on which I received revelation. (Muslim)

'Abdullah ibn 'Amr ibn al-'Âṣ (ﷺ) reported that the Messenger of Allah (ﷺ) said: «Fasting on three days during the month is equivalent to a full month of fasting.» (Bukhari and Muslim)

Zayd ibn Khâlid al-Juhani (ﷺ) reported that the Prophet (ﷺ) said: «He who provides a fasting person something with which to break his fast will earn the same reward as the one who was observing the fast, without diminishing in any way the reward of the latter.» (a sound hadith recorded by at-Tirmidhi)

Virtues of dhikr (Remembrance of Allah)

Abu Hurayrah (ﷺ) reported that the Messenger of Allah (ﷺ) said: «Allah (ﷺ) says: I am as my slave expects me to be, and I am with him when he remembers Me. If he remembers Me inwardly, I will remember him inwardly, and if he remembers Me in an assembly, I will remember him in a better assembly (meaning the assembly of angels).» (Bukhari and Muslim)

«'Abdullah ibn Busr (ﷺ) reported that one of the Companions said: O Messenger of Allah, there are many injunctions of Islam for me, so tell me something to which I may hold fast. He (ﷺ) said: Keep your tongue wet with the remembrance of Allah (ﷺ).» (a sound hadith recorded by at-Tirmidhi)

Abu Moosâ al-Ash'ari (ﷺ) reported that the Prophet (ﷺ) said: «The similitude of one who remembers his Lord and one who does not remember Him is like that of the living and the dead.» (Bukhari and Muslim)

Abu Hurayrah (رضي الله عنه) reported that the Messenger of Allah (ﷺ) said: «There are two statements that are light for the tongue to remember, heavy on the scales, and dear to the Merciful: *subhânallâhi wa bihamdih* (glory be to Allah, and His is the praise) and *subhânallâhil-Adheem* (glory be to Allah the Most Great).» (Bukhari and Muslim)

Abu Hurayrah (رضي الله عنه) reported that the Messenger of Allah (ﷺ) said: «The uttering of the words: *subhânallâh* (glory be to Allah), *alhamdulillâh* (all praise is for Allah), *lâ ilâha illâ Allâh* (there is none worthy of worship other than Allah) and *Allâhu akbar* (Allah is the Greatest) is dearer to me than anything over which the sun rises.» (Muslim)

Abu Ayyoob al-Ansâri (رضي الله عنه) reported that the Prophet (ﷺ) said: «He who utters ten times: *lâ ilâha illâ Allâh wahdahu lâ shareeka lahu, lahul mulku wa lahul hamdu, wa Huwa 'alâ kulli shay'in Qadeer* (there is none worthy of worship other than Allah alone, who has no partner; His is the dominion and His is the praise, and He is All-Powerful over all things), he will have a reward equal to that of freeing four slaves from the descendants of Prophet Ismâ'eel (عليه السلام).» (Bukhari and Muslim)

Abu Dharr (رضي الله عنه) reported that the Messenger of Allah (ﷺ) said to him: «Shall I tell you the expression that is most loved by Allah? It is: *subhânallâhi wa bihamdih* (glory be to Allah, and His is the praise).» (Muslim)

Abu Mâlik al-Ash'ari (رضي الله عنه) reported that the Messenger of Allah (ﷺ) said: «Ablution is half of prayer, and the expression *subhânallâh* (glory be to Allah) fills the scale, and the expression *alhamdulillâh* (all praise is for Allah) fills the space between the heavens and the earth.» (Muslim)

Abu Hurayrah (ﷺ) reported that the Messenger of Allah (ﷺ) said: «He who recites after every prayer: *subḥânallâh* (glory be to Allah) thirty-three times; *alḥamdulillâh* (all praise is for Allah) thirty-three times; *Allâhu akbar* (Allah is the Greatest) thirty-three times; and completes the hundred with: *Lâ ilâha illâ Allâh waḥdahu lâ shareeka lahu, lahul mulku wa lahul ḥamdu, wa Huwa 'alâ kulli shay'in Qadeer* (There is none worthy of worship other than Allah alone, who has no partner. His is the dominion and His is the praise, and He is All-Powerful over all things), will have all his sins pardoned even if they are as much as the foam on the surface of the sea.» (Muslim)

«Sa'd ibn Abi Waqqâṣ (ﷺ) reported: We were with the Messenger of Allah (ﷺ) when he asked: Is any one of you unable to earn a thousand good deeds? One of those present asked: How can one earn thousand good deeds in a day?' He (ﷺ) replied: By saying *subḥânallâh* (glory be to Allah) a hundred times, then one thousand good deeds will be recorded, and one thousand sins will be blotted out.» (Muslim)

Abu Dharr (ﷺ) reported that the Messenger of Allah (ﷺ) said: «Every morning, charity is due from every bone in the body of everyone of you. Every utterance of Allah's glorification (*subḥânallâh*) is an act of charity, every utterance of praise of Him (*alḥamdulillâh*) is an act of charity, every utterance of the profession of faith (*lâ ilâha illâ Allâh*) is an act of charity, every utterance of His greatness (*Allâhu akbar*) is an act of charity; enjoining good is an act of charity, and forbidding what is disreputable is an act of charity. The two unit prayer that one offers in the mid-morning, before noon, will suffice for all this.» (Muslim)

Jâbir (ﷺ) reported that he heard the Messenger of Allah (ﷺ) saying: «The best way to celebrate the remembrance of Allah (ﷺ) is to say: *lâ ilâha illâ Allâh* (there is none worthy of worship other than Allah).» (a reliable hadith recorded by at-Tirmidhi)

«Abu Moosâ al-Ash'ari (ﷺ) reported: The Messenger of Allah (ﷺ) said to me: Shall I not guide you to a treasure from the treasures of paradise? I said: Yes, O Messenger of Allah! Thereupon he (ﷺ) said: (Recite) *Lâ ḥawla wa lâ quwwata illâ billâh* (There is no might and no power except in Allah).» (Bukhari and Muslim)

'Abdullah ibn 'Amr ibn al-'Âṣ (ﷺ) reported that he heard the Messenger of Allah (ﷺ) saying: «Whoever supplicates Allah (ﷺ) to exalt my mention, Allah (ﷺ) will exalt his mention ten times.» (Muslim)

Ibn Mas'ood (ﷺ) reported that the Messenger of Allah (ﷺ) said: «The people who will be nearest to me on the Day of Resurrection will be those who supplicate Allah (ﷺ) more often for me.» (a reliable hadith recorded by at-Tirmidhi)

Abu Hurayrah (ﷺ) reported that the Messenger of Allah (ﷺ) said: «Allah (ﷺ) makes the way to paradise easy for one who treads the path in search of knowledge.» (Muslim)

«...Abu Dharr (ﷺ) goes on saying that he asked for more advice. The Messenger of Allah (ﷺ) advised him that he should cultivate fear of Allah (ﷺ) because it is the root and basis of all spiritual actions. Abu Dharr (ﷺ) then begged for more advice. The Messenger of Allah (ﷺ) said: Be consistent in recitation of the Qur'an and in remembrance of Allah, because it is illumination in this world and a means of intercession on your behalf in the hereafter. Abu Dharr again sought further advice and was told: Abstain from too much laughter, because it causes the heart to wither, and the face loses its lustre. Abu Dharr sought further advice, whereupon the Messenger of Allah (ﷺ) said: Stick to jihad, because this is the monasticism for my Ummah. Abu Dharr asked for more advice, and the Messenger of Allah (ﷺ) said: Associate yourself with the poor and the needy, be friendly with them and sit in their company. When Abu Dharr (﵁) requested further advice, the Messenger of Allah (ﷺ) said: Look towards those who rank below you, so that you may get used to being thankful, and do not look at those who rank above you, lest you should despise the favours of Allah (ﷻ) upon you. When Abu Dharr again asked for more advice, the Messenger of Allah (ﷺ) said: Say the truth even if it is bitter. He again asked for more advice, and the Messenger of Allah (ﷺ) said: Do not fear in Allah (ﷻ) the censuring of any censurer.» (a sound hadith recorded by Ibn Ḥibbân)

CONCLUSION

The blessing that we Muslims have is that we have all of the answers to our problems. Most non-Muslims that I see have many problems that they cannot solve because they do not know why they are occurring in the first place. Instead, they get angry and frustrated and turn to things that exacerbate their problems (without even realizing that those things are making the problems worse). They use a variety of defense mechanisms and turn to a variety of distractions.

The Prophet (ﷺ) taught us the causes of all problems, as well as how to prevent them and solve them. The answer is simple. All we have to do is follow the Sunnah, and most of the issues we have will go away.

If we follow Islam through the Sunnah, we will be happy and experience inner peace. We will have happy marriages, happy families, and happy households. We will have mosques that the ordinary Muslims want to visit. We will have the best neighbourhoods. Many non-Muslims will enter the fold of Islam. We will have dignity and strength on the earth, and its wealth will be given to us.

This book is just as much a reminder to myself as it is to the readers. I need the advice given here just as much as you do, if not more. Anything correct that I have said in this book is from Allah (ﷻ), as He is our guide, and anything incorrect that I have said is from myself and from Satan. I ask any readers who have benefited from this book to make supplications for me and keep me in your prayers. Ask Allah (ﷻ) to forgive my sins, save my family and me from the hellfire and the punishment in the grave, and grant us a high station in the highest heaven in paradise. Ask Allah (ﷻ) to guide my parents, grandparents, sisters, in-laws, aunts, uncles and cousins on the path to paradise and away from the path to hell. Ask Allah (ﷻ) to give me the good in this life and in the hereafter. Ask Allah (ﷻ) to make me desire only that which is good and to give me all of that.

If you would like to contact me, please write to the publisher, who will forward your mail or e-mail to me, insha Allah.

BIBLIOGRAPHY

ali-'Ubaykaan, 'Abdul-Muhsin ibn Naasir. *The Khawaarij & Their Recurring Ideologies*. Translated by Abu az-Zubayr Harrison. Dallas, Texas: Tarbiyyah Bookstore Publishing and Distribution.

Bukhari, Muhammad ibn Ismâ'eel. *Sahih al-Bukhari: Translation of the Meanings*. Translated by Muhammad Muhsin Khan. Riyadh: Dar-us-Salam Publications, 1997.

—————. *Imam Bukhari's Book of Muslim Morals and Manners*. Translated by Yusuf Talal de Lorenzo. Alexandria, VA: Al-Saadawi Publications, 1997.

Ember, Carol R. and Melvin Ember. *Cultural Anthropology (Ninth Edition)*. Upper Saddle River, NJ: Prentice Hall, 1999.

Al-Fawzan, Dr. Salih. *A Summary of Islamic Jurisprudence, Volumes 1-2*. Riyadh: Al-Maiman Publishing House, 2005.

Fisher, Helen. *Anatomy of Love: A Natural History of Mating, Marriage, and Why We Stray*. New York: Ballantine Books, 1994.

Hadith: Charity. http://www.islamawareness.net/Hadith/htopic_charity.html (accessed on November 11, 2009).

Hallaq, Muhammad Subhi bin Hasan. *Fiqh According to the Qur'an and Sunnah*. Riyadh: Dar-us-Salam Publications, 2007.

Ibn Katheer, Ismâ'eel ibn Omar. *The Signs Before the Day of Judgment (With Website Amendments).* Translated by Huda Khattab. http://www.sunnahonline.com/ilm/unseen/0002.htm (accessed on November 11, 2009).

Ibn Rushd. *The Distinguished Jurist's Primer Volume I: Bidayat al-Mujtahid wa Nihayat al-Muqtasid.* Translated by Imran Ahsan Khan Nyazee. Garnet Publishing, Ltd., 1994.

————. *The Distinguished Jurist's Primer Volume II: Bidayat al-Mujtahid wa Nihayat al-Muqtasid.* Translated by Imran Ahsan Khan Nyazee. Garnet Publishing, Ltd., 1996.

Khalid, M. *Men around the Messenger.* Translated by M. Sharif. Beirut: Dar al-Kotob al-Ilmiyah, 2005.

Jessel, David and Dr. Anne Moir. *Brain Sex.* New York: Dell Publishing, 1989.

al-Munajjid, M. *I Want to Repent, But...* Riyadh: International Islamic Publishing House, 2006.

Muslim, Imam. *Sahih Muslim.* Translated by Abdul Hamid Siddiqui. New Delhi: Kitab Bhavan, 2000.

An-Nawawi, Yahya ibn Sharaf. *Riyad-us-Saliheen.* Translated by Salahuddin Yusuf. Riyadh: Dar-us-Salam Publications, 1999.

Philips, Bilal. *Tafseer of Soorat al-Ḥujurât.* Riyadh: International Islamic Publishing House, 2006.

Al-Qahtâni, Sa'eed ibn 'Ali ibn Wahf, comp. *Husnal Muslim Min Adhkar al-Kitab was Sunnah (Fortification of the Muslim through Remembrance and Supplication from the Qur'aan and the Sunnah).* Riyadh: Safir Press. http://www.makedua.com (accessed on November 12, 2009).

Sabiq, Sayyid. *Fiqh us Sunnah.* Indianapolis: American Trust Publications, 1992.

Al-Sadlaan, Dr. Saalih ibn Ghaanim. *Marital Discord (al-Nushooz): Its Definition, Cases, Causes, Means of Protection from it, and its Remedy from the Qur'an and Sunnah.* Translated by Jamal al-Din M. Zarabozo. Boulder, Co: Al-Basheer Publications and Translations, 1996.

——————. *The Fiqh of Marriage According to the Qur'an and Sunnah.* Translated by Jamal al-Din M. Zarabozo. Boulder, Co: Al-Basheer Publications and Translations, 1999.

Safi, Louay. *Peace and the Limits of War: Transcending the Classical Conception of Jihad.* Herndon, Va.: The International Institute of Islamic Thought, 2003.

Salafi Publications. *The Islamic Condemnation of Terrorists, Hijackers, & Suicide Bombers: The Brothers of Devils.* Birmingham, UK: Salafi Publications, 2001.

Sallâbi, A.M. *'Umar ibn al-Khattâb: His Life and Times.* Riyadh: International Islamic Publishing House, 2007.

Shakir, Imam Zaid. *Scattered Pictures: Reflections of an American Muslim.* Hayward, CA: Zaytuna Institute, 2005.

Siddiqui, Dr. Muzammil H. *Islam and Non-Muslims, Girls and Sports.* http://www.pakistanlink.com/religion/97/re09-26-97.html (accessed on November 10, 2009).

Wood, David. "Effect of child and family poverty on child health in the United States." *Pediatrics* 112 (2003). http://pediatrics.aappublications.org/cgi/content/full/112/3/S1/707 (accessed April 2004).

APPENDIX

Supplications said in the morning and the evening

أَصْبَحْنَا وَأَصْبَحَ الْمُلْكُ لِلَّهِ وَالْحَمْدُ لِلَّهِ، لاَ إِلَهَ إِلاَّ اللَّهُ وَحْدَهُ لاَ شَرِيكَ لَهُ،

لَهُ الْمُلْكُ وَلَهُ الْحَمْدُ وَهُوَ عَلَى كُلِّ شَيْءٍ قَدِيرٌ،

رَبِّ أَسْأَلُكَ خَيْرَ مَا فِي هَذَا الْيَوْمِ وَخَيْرَ مَا بَعْدَهُ،

وَأَعُوذُ بِكَ مِنْ شَرِّ مَا فِي هَذَا الْيَوْمِ وَشَرِّ مَا بَعْدَهُ، رَبِّ أَعُوذُ بِكَ مِنَ الْكَسَلِ،

وَسُوءِ الْكِبَرِ، رَبِّ أَعُوذُ بِكَ مِنْ عَذَابٍ فِي النَّارِ وَعَذَابٍ فِي الْقَبْرِ

In the morning, say, "*Aṣbaḥnâ wa aṣbaḥal-mulku lillâhi walḥamdu lillâhi, lâ ilâha illa Allâhu waḥdahu lâ shareeka lahu, lahul-mulku wa lahul-ḥamdu wa huwa 'alâ kulli shay'in Qadeer, Rabbi asaluka khayra mâ fee **hâdhal-yawma**, wa khayra mâ ba'dahu, wa a'oodhu bika min sharri **hâdhal-yawma** wa sharri mâ ba'dahu, Rabbi a'oodhu bika minal-kasali, wa soo'il-kibari, Rabbi a'oodhu bika min 'adhâbin fin-nâri wa 'adhâbin fil-qabr.* [We have reached the **morning**, and at this very time unto Allah belongs all sovereignty, and all praise is for Allah. None has the right to be worshipped except Allah alone, without partner. To Him belongs all sovereignty and praise, and He is All-Powerful over all things. My Lord, I ask for the good of this **day** and the good of what follows it, and I seek refuge in You from the evil of this **day** and the evil of what follows it. My

Lord, I seek refuge in You from laziness and senility. My Lord, I seek refuge in You from torment in the fire and punishment in the grave]."[78]

أَمْسَيْنَا وَ أَمْسَى الْمُلْكُ لِلَّهِ وَالْحَمْدُ لِلَّهِ، لاَ إِلَهَ إِلاَّ اللَّهُ وَحْدَهُ لاَ شَرِيكَ لَهُ،

لَهُ الْمُلْكُ وَلَهُ الْحَمْدُ وَهُوَ عَلَى كُلِّ شَيْءٍ قَدِيرٌ،

رَبِّ أَسْأَلُكَ خَيْرَ مَا فِي هَذِهِ اللَّيْلَةِ وَخَيْرَ مَا بَعْدَهُ،

وَأَعُوذُ بِكَ مِنْ شَرِّ مَا فِي هَذِهِ اللَّيْلَةِ وَشَرِّ مَا بَعْدَهُ، رَبِّ أَعُوذُ بِكَ مِنَ الْكَسَلِ،

وَسُوءِ الْكِبَرِ، رَبِّ أَعُوذُ بِكَ مِنْ عَذَابٍ فِي النَّارِ وَعَذَابٍ فِي الْقَبْرِ

In the evening, say: "*Amsaynâ wa amsiyal-mulku lillâhi walḥamdu lillâhi, lâ ilâha illa Allâhu waḥdahu lâ shareeka lahu, lahul-mulku wa lahul-ḥamdu wa huwa 'alâ kulli shay'in Qadeer, Rabbi asaluka khayra mâ fee hâdhihil-laylah, wa khayra mâ ba'dahâ, wa a'oodhu bika min sharri hâdhihil-laylah wa sharri mâ ba'dahâ, Rabbi a'oodhu bika minal-kasali, wa soo'il-kibari, Rabbi a'oodhu bika min 'adhâbin fin-nâri wa 'adhâbin fil-qabr.* [We have reached the **evening**, and at this very time all sovereignty belongs to Allah, and all praise is for Allah. None has the right to be worshipped except Allah alone, without partner. To Him belongs all sovereignty and praise, and He is All-Powerful over all things. My Lord, I ask for the good of this **night** and the good of what follows it, and I seek refuge in You from the evil of this **night** and the evil of what follows it. My Lord, I seek refuge in You from laziness and senility. My Lord, I seek refuge in You from torment in the fire and punishment in the grave]." (Muslim)

---

[78] The English translations of many of the supplications in this section have been adapted from those found at www.makedua.com.

اللَّهُمَّ بِكَ أَصْبَحْنَا، وَبِكَ أَمْسَيْنَا، وَبِكَ نَحْيَا، وَبِكَ نَمُوتُ وَإِلَيْكَ النُّشُورُ

In the morning, say, "*Allâhumma bika aṣbaḥnâ, wa bika amsaynâ, wa bika naḥyâ wa bika namootu, wa 'ilaykan-nushoor.* [O Allah, by your leave, we have reached the morning, and by Your leave, we have reached the evening. By Your leave, we live and die, and unto You is our resurrection]."

اللَّهُمَّ بِكَ أَمْسَيْنَا، وَبِكَ أَصْبَحْنَا، وَبِكَ نَحْيَا، وَبِكَ نَمُوتُ وَإِلَيْكَ المَصِيرُ

In the evening, say, "*Allâhumma bika amsaynâ, wa bika aṣbaḥnâ, wa bika naḥyâ wa bika namootu, wa 'ilaykal-maṣeer.* [O Allah, by Your leave, we have reached the evening, and by Your leave we have reached the morning. By Your leave, we live and die, and unto You is our return]." (from a sound hadith recorded by at-Tirmidhi)

اللَّهُمَّ أَنْتَ رَبِّي لاَ إِلَهَ إِلاَّ أَنْتَ، خَلَقْتَنِي وَأَنَا عَبْدُكَ، وَأَنَا عَلَى عَهْدِكَ
وَوَعْدِكَ مَا اسْتَطَعْتُ، أَعُوذُ بِكَ مِنْ شَرِّ مَا صَنَعْتُ، أَبُوءُ لَكَ بِنِعْمَتِكَ عَلَيَّ،
وَأَبُوءُ بِذَنْبِي فَاغْفِرْ لِي فَإِنَّهُ لاَ يَغْفِرُ الذُّنُوبَ إِلاَّ أَنْتَ

Say, "*Allâhumma anta rabbee lâ ilâha illâ anta khalaqtanee wa anâ 'abduka, wa anâ 'alâ 'ahdika wa wa'dika mas-taṭa'tu, a'oodhu bika min sharri mâ ṣana'tu, aboo'u laka bini'matika 'alayya, wa aboo'u bidhanbee, faghfir lee fa-innahu lâ yaghfirudh-dhunooba illâ anta.* [O Allah, You are my Lord; none has the right to be worshipped except You. You created me; I am Your servant, and I abide by Your covenant and promise as best I can. I seek refuge in You from the evil which I committed. I acknowledge Your favour upon me, and I acknowledge my sin, so forgive me, for verily none can forgive sin except You]." (Bukhari, an-Nasâ'i and at-Tirmidhi)

اللَّهُمَّ إِنِّي أَصْبَحْتُ أُشْهِدُكَ وَأُشْهِدُ حَمَلَةَ عَرْشِكَ،
وَمَلَائِكَتَكَ وَجَمِيعَ خَلْقِكَ، أَنَّكَ أَنْتَ اللَّهُ لاَ إِلَهَ إِلاَّ أَنْتَ
وَحْدَكَ لاَ شَرِيكَ لَكَ، وَأَنَّ مُحَمَّداً عَبْدُكَ وَرَسُولُكَ

In the morning, say four times, "*Allâhumma innee aṣbaḥtu ush-hiduka, wa ush-hidu ḥamalata 'arshika, wa malâ'ikataka, wajamee'a khalqika, annaka antallâhu lâ ilâha illâ anta, waḥdaka lâ shareeka laka, wa anna muḥammadan 'abduka wa rasooluka.* [O Allah, verily I have reached the **morning** and call on You, the bearers of Your throne, Your angels, and all of Your creation to witness that You are Allah, none has the right to be worshipped except You alone, without partner, and that Muhammad is Your servant and Messenger]."

اللَّهُمَّ إِنِّي أَمْسَيْتُ أُشْهِدُكَ وَأُشْهِدُ حَمَلَةَ عَرْشِكَ،
وَمَلَائِكَتَكَ وَجَمِيعَ خَلْقِكَ، أَنَّكَ أَنْتَ اللَّهُ لاَ إِلَهَ إِلاَّ أَنْتَ
وَحْدَكَ لاَ شَرِيكَ لَكَ، وَأَنَّ مُحَمَّداً عَبْدُكَ وَرَسُولُكَ

In the evening, say four times, "*Allâhumma innee amsaytu ush-hiduka, wa ush-hidu ḥamalata 'arshika, wa malâ'ikataka, wajamee'a khalqika, annaka antallâhu lâ ilâha illâ anta, waḥdaka lâ shareeka laka, wa anna muḥammadan 'abduka wa rasooluka.* [O Allah, verily I have reached the **evening** and call on You, the bearers of Your throne, Your angels, and all of Your creation to witness that You are Allah, none has the right to be worshipped except You alone, without partner, and that Muhammad is Your servant and Messenger]." (Bukhari)

اللَّهُمَّ مَا أَصْبَحَ بِي مِنْ نِعْمَةٍ أَوْ بِأَحَدٍ مِنْ خَلْقِكَ فَمِنْكَ
وَحْدَكَ لاَ شَرِيكَ لَكَ، فَلَكَ الْحَمْدُ وَلَكَ الشُّكْرُ

In the morning, say, "*Allâhumma mâ aṣbaḥa bee min niʿmatin, aw bi-aḥadin min khalqika, faminka waḥdaka lâ shareeka laka, falakal-ḥamdu wa lakash-shukru.* [O Allah, any blessing that I, or any of Your creation, have reached the **morning** with is from You alone, without partner, so for You is all praise and unto You all thanks]."

اللَّهُمَّ مَا أَمْسَى بِي مِنْ نِعْمَةٍ أَوْ بِأَحَدٍ مِنْ خَلْقِكَ فَمِنْكَ
وَحْدَكَ لاَ شَرِيكَ لَكَ، فَلَكَ الْحَمْدُ وَلَكَ الشُّكْرُ

In the evening, say, "*Allâhumma mâ amsa bee min niʿmatin, aw bi-aḥadin min khalqika, faminka waḥdaka lâ shareeka laka, falakal-ḥamdu wa lakash-shukru.* [O Allah, any blessing that I, or any of Your creation, have reached the **evening** with is from You alone, without partner, so for You is all praise and unto You all thanks]."

Whoever says this in the morning has indeed offered his thanks for the day, and whoever says this in the evening has indeed offered his thanks for the night. (from a sound hadith recorded by Abu Dâwood and an-Nasâ'i)

اللَّهُمَّ عَافِنِي فِي بَدَنِي، اللَّهُمَّ عَافِنِي فِي سَمْعِي،
اللَّهُمَّ عَافِنِي فِي بَصَرِي، لا إِلَهَ إِلاَّ أَنْتَ

Say three times, "*Allâhumma ʿâfinee fee badanee, allâhumma ʿâfinee fee samʿee, allâhumma ʿâfinee fee baṣaree, lâ ilâha illâ anta.* [O Allah, grant my body health. O Allah, grant my hearing health. O Allah, grant my sight health. None has the right to be worshipped except You]." (Bukhari, Abu Dâwood, Aḥmad and an-Nasâ'i)

اللّهُـمَّ إنّي أَعـوذُ بِكَ مِنَ الْكُفرِ، وَالفَـقْرِ،

وَأَعـوذُ بِكَ مِنْ عَذابِ القَبْرِ، لا إلَهَ إلاّ أَنْـتَ

Say three times, "*Allâhumma innee a'oodhu bika minal-kufri, walfaqri, wa a'oodhu bika min 'adhâbil-qabri, lâ ilâha illâ anta.* [O Allah, I take refuge with You from disbelief and poverty, and I take refuge with You from the punishment of the grave. None has the right to be worshipped except You]." (Bukhari, Abu Dâwood, Aḥmad and an-Nasâ'i)

حَسْبِيَ اللّهُ لاَ إلَهَ إلاّ هُوَ عَلَيْهِ تَوَكَّلْتُ وَهُوَ رَبُّ الْعَرْشِ الْعَظِيمِ

Say seven times, in the morning and evening, "*Ḥasbiyallâhu lâ ilâha illâ huwa 'alayhi tawakkaltu wa huwa rabbul-'arshil-'adheem.* [Allah is sufficient for me. None has the right to be worshipped except Him. Upon Him I rely, and He is Lord of the exalted throne]." (from a sound hadith recorded by Abu Dâwood and Ibn as-Sunni)

أَعُوذُ بِكَلِمَاتِ اللّهِ التَّامَّاتِ مِنْ شَرِّ مَا خَلَقَ

Say three times, "*A'oodhu bikalimâtil-lâhit-tâmmâti min sharri mâ khalaq.* [I seek refuge in the perfect words of Allah from the evil He has created]." (from a sound hadith recorded by Ibn Mâjah)

اللَّهُمَّ عَالِمَ الْغَيْبِ وَالشَّهَادَةِ فَاطِرَ السَّماوَاتِ وَالْأَرْضِ،

رَبَّ كُلِّ شَيْءٍ وَمَلِيكَهُ، أَشْهَدُ أَنْ لاَ إلَهَ إلاّ أَنْتَ، أَعُوذُ بِكَ مِنْ شَرِّ نَفْسِي،

وَمِنْ شَرِّ الشَّيْطَانِ وَشِرْكِهِ، وَأَنْ أَقْتَرِفَ عَلَى نَفْسِي سُوءاً، أَوْ أَجُرَّهُ إلَى مُسْلِمٍ

Say, "*Allâhumma 'âlimal-ghaybi wash-shahâdati fâṭiras-samawâti wal-arḍi rabba kulli shay'in wa maleekahu, ash-hadu an lâ ilâha illâ anta, a'oodhu bika min sharri nafsee wa min sharrish-shayṭâni wa shirkihi, wa an aqtarifa 'alâ nafsee soo'an, aw ajurrahu ilâ muslimin.*

[O Allah, Knower of the unseen and the seen, Creator of the heavens and the earth, Lord and Sovereign of all things, I bear witness that none has the right to be worshipped except You. I seek refuge in You from the evil of my soul and from the evil and shirk of the devil, and from committing wrong against my soul or bringing such upon another Muslim]." (from a sound hadith recorded by at-Tirmidhi and Abu Dâwood)

$$ بِسْمِ اللَّهِ الَّذِي لاَ يَضُرُّ مَعَ اسْمِهِ شَيْءٌ فِي الْأَرْضِ $$
$$ وَلاَ فِي السَّمَاءِ وَهُوَ السَّمِيعُ الْعَلِيمُ $$

Say three times, "*Bismillâhil-ladhee lâ yaḍurru ma'as-mihi shay'un fil-arḍi wa lâ fis-samâ'i wa huwas-samee'ul-'aleem.* [In the name of Allah, with whose name nothing is harmed on earth or in the heavens. He is the All-Hearing, the All-Knowing]." (from a reliable hadith recorded by Abu Dâwood, at-Tirmidhi, Ibn Mâjah and Aḥmad)

$$ رَضِيتُ بِاللَّهِ رَبَّاً، وَبِالْإِسْلاَمِ دِيناً، وَبِمُحَمَّدٍ صَلَّى اللَّهُ عَلَيهِ وَسَلَّمَ نَبِيّاً $$

Say three times, "*Raḍeetu billâhi rabban wa bil-islâmi deenan, wa bi-muḥammadin (ṣallallâhu 'alayhi wa sallam) nabiyyan.* [I am pleased with Allah as a Lord, Islam as a religion and Muhammad (ﷺ) as a Prophet]." (from a reliable hadith recorded by Aḥmad, an-Nasâ'i, Ibn as-Sunni and at-Tirmidhi)

$$ سُبْحَانَ اللَّهِ وَبِحَمْدِهِ: عَدَدَ خَلْقِهِ، وَرِضَى نَفْسِهِ، وَزِنَةَ عَرْشِهِ وَمِدَادَ كَلِمَاتِهِ $$

Say three times, "*Subḥânallâhi wa biḥamdihi 'adada khalqihi wa riḍâ nafsihi wa zinata 'arshihi wa midâda kalimâtihi.* [Glory to Allah, and His is the praise by the number of His creation and His pleasure, and by the weight of His throne and the ink of His words]." (Muslim)

$$\text{سُبْحَانَ اللَّهِ وَبِحَمْدِهِ}$$

Say one hundred times, "*Subḥânallâhi wa biḥamdihi*. [Glory to Allah, and His is the praise]." (Bukhari)

$$\text{يَا حَيُّ يَا قَيُّومُ بِرَحْمَتِكَ أَسْتَغِيثُ أَصْلِحْ لِي شَأْنِي كُلَّهُ}$$
$$\text{وَلاَ تَكِلْنِي إِلَى نَفْسِي طَرْفَةَ عَيْنٍ}$$

Say, "*Yâ ḥayyu yâ qayyoomu biraḥmatika astagheethu aṣliḥ lee sha'nee kullahu wa lâ takilnee ilâ nafsee ṭarfata 'aynin.* [O Ever-Living, O Self-Subsisting and Supporter of all, by Your mercy I seek assistance. Rectify for me all of my affairs and do not leave me to myself, even for the blink of an eye]." (from a sound hadith recorded by al-Hâkim)

$$\text{لاَ إِلَهَ إِلاَّ اللَّهُ وَحْدَهُ لاَ شَرِيكَ لَهُ، لَهُ الْمُلْكُ وَلَهُ الْحَمْدُ،}$$
$$\text{وَهُوَ عَلَى كُلِّ شَيْءٍ قَدِيرٌ}$$

The Messenger of Allah (ﷺ) said: «Whoever says in the morning: *Lâ ilaha illallâhu waḥdahu lâ shareeka lahu, lahul-mulku wa lahul-ḥamdu, wa Huwa 'alâ kulli shay'in Qadeer* [There is none worthy of worship other than Allah alone, Who has no partner. His is the dominion and His is the praise, and He is All-Powerful over all things], has indeed gained the reward of freeing a slave from the children of Ismâ'eel. Ten of his sins are wiped away, he is raised ten degrees, and he has found a safe retreat from the devil until evening. Similarly, if he says it at evening time, he will be protected until the morning.» (a sound hadith recorded by Ibn Mâjah)

Recite this one hundred times, in Arabic, upon rising in the morning. Abu Hurayrah (ﷺ) reported that the Messenger of Allah (ﷺ) said: «He who utters one hundred times a day these words: *Lâ ilaha illallâhu waḥdahu lâ shareeka lahu, lahul-mulku wa lahul-*

ḥamdu, wa Huwa 'alâ kulli shay'in Qadeer [There is none worthy of worship other than Allah alone, Who has no partner. His is the dominion and His is the praise, and He is All-Powerful over all things], will have a reward equivalent to that of emancipating ten slaves, one hundred good deeds will be recorded to his credit, one hundred of his sins will be blotted out from his scroll, and he will be safeguarded against the devil on that day until the evening. No one brings anything more excellent than this except someone who has recited these words more often than him and has done more good deeds. He who utters: *Subḥânallâhi wa biḥamdih* [Glory be to Allah, and His is the praise] one hundred times a day, his sins will be obliterated, even if they are equal to the extent of the foam of the ocean.» (Bukhari and Muslim)

أَصْبَحْنَا عَلَى فِطْرَةِ الْإِسْلَام وَعَلَى كَلِمَةِ الْإِخْلَاصِ،
وَعَلَى دِينِ نَبِيِّنَا مُحَمَّدٍ صَلَّى اللَّهُ عَلِيهِ وَسَلَّمَ، وَعَلَى مِلَّةِ أَبِينَا إِبْرَاهِيمَ،
حَنِيفَاً مُسْلِماً وَمَا كَانَ مِنَ الْمُشْرِكِينَ

In the morning, say, *"Aṣbaḥnâ 'alâ fiṭratil-Islâm, wa 'alâ kalimatil-ikhlâṣi, wa 'alâ deeni nabiyyinâ muḥammadin (ṣallallâhu 'alayhi wa sallam), wa 'alâ milliti abeenâ ibrâheema ḥaneefan musliman wa mâ kâna minal-mushrikeen.* [We **rise in the morning** on the fiṭrah of Islam, and the word of pure faith, and following the religion of our Prophet Muhammad (ﷺ) and the religion of our forefather Abraham, who was a Muslim and of true faith, and was not of those who associate others with Allah].*"

أَمْسَيْنَا عَلَى فِطْرَةِ الْإِسْلَام وَعَلَى كَلِمَةِ الْإِخْلَاصِ،
وَعَلَى دِينِ نَبِيِّنَا مُحَمَّدٍ صَلَّى اللَّهُ عَلِيهِ وَسَلَّمَ، وَعَلَى مِلَّةِ أَبِينَا إِبْرَاهِيمَ،
حَنِيفَاً مُسْلِماً وَمَا كَانَ مِنَ الْمُشْرِكِينَ

When you say this in the evening, you should say: "*Amsaynâ 'alâ fiṭratil-Islâm, wa 'alâ kalimatil-ikhlâṣi, wa 'alâ deeni nabiyyinâ muḥammadin (ṣallallâhu 'alayhi wa sallam), wa 'alâ milliti abeenâ ibrâheema ḥaneefan musliman wa mâ kâna minal-mushrikeen. [We reach the evening on the fiṭrah of Islam, and the word of pure faith, and following the religion of our Prophet Muhammad (ﷺ) and the religion of our forefather Abraham, who was a Muslim and of true faith, and was not of those who associate others with Allah].*"

Recite the last three chapters of the Qur'an. «'Abdullah ibn Khubaib (ﷺ) said: The Messenger of Allah (ﷺ) said to me: Recite! I replied: O Messenger of Allah, what shall I recite? He said: Recite soorat al-Ikhlâṣ, soorat al-Falaq and soorat an-Nâs, in the evening and the morning three times, for it will suffice you of all else.» (a sound hadith recorded by an-Nasâ'i)

GLOSSARY OF ISLAMIC TERMS*

abu (or abi) أبو، أبي father (of)

alḥamdulillâh الحمد لله all praise is for Allah

Allâhu akbar الله أكبر Allah is the Greatest

âmeen آمين O Allah, accept our invocation; amen

angel A being made of light who is totally obedient to Allah and has no free will; Allah has assigned some angels specific tasks, like those who record our good and bad deeds, the Angel of Death, the guardians of hell, etc.

Anṣâr أنصار 'helpers': the Muslim citizens of Madinah who gave refuge to the Prophet (ﷺ) and the other Muslim emigrants from Makkah

as-salâmu 'alaykum السلام عليكم a greeting, which means 'peace'

bismillâh بسم الله in the name of Allah

Dajjâl الدجّال Antichrist (anti-Christ)

---

* The Arabic words are transliterated according to the conventions of the Transliteration Chart found in this book. If a word has become part of the English language (i.e., is found in a dictionary of Standard English), that spelling is used in this book and appears first in this Glossary, with the transliterated form in brackets after it.

dhikr Allâh	ذكر الله	remembrance of Allah; specifically, remembering Allah through praising and supplicating to Him
dhimmi	ذمّي	protected or covenanted people; non-Muslims who must pay the jizyah in lieu of zakât
dinar (deenâr)	دينار	originally, a gold coin; a unit of currency
dirham	درهم	a silver coin; a unit of currency
dunyâ	دونيا	the material world
eemân	إيمان	faith; belief in all the six pillars of the creed of Islam
Eid ('eed)	عيد	*lit.* festival; the two celebrations: one at the end of Ramadan and the other at the culmination of the Hajj
fiqh	فقه	Islamic jurisprudence; understanding or interpreting Islamic law
fitnah	فتنة	*lit.* trial, temptation; (attempting to sow) discord between Muslims
fitrah	فطرة	the natural inclination (of humans) instilled by Allah
ghusl	غسل	ritual shower necessary after a major impurity, e.g., after sexual intercourse or at the end of the menstrual period
Hadith (hadeeth)	حديث	the collected statements and actions of Prophet Muhammad (ﷺ) that with the Qur'an form the basis of Islamic law
hadith (hadeeth)	حديث	a statement or action of Prophet Muhammad (ﷺ) that was remembered and recorded by his Companions and followers

Hajj (ḥajj)	حج	the major pilgrimage to the Sacred Mosque, site of the Ka'bah at Makkah, to be undertaken by every able Muslim once in his/her lifetime
Ḥijâz	حجاز	the Western region of the Arabian Peninsula that includes Makkah and Madinah
ijtihâd	إجتهاد	to use one's knowledge of the Qur'an and the Sunnah to derive rulings on matters not specifically mentioned in either source of Islamic law
inshallah (in shâ'Allah)	أن شاءالله	God willing
istikhârah	إستخارة	a prayer by which one seeks guidance from Allah
jâhiliyah	جاهلية	*lit.* 'ignorance'; the age of spiritual darkness before Islam
Jibreel	جبريل	the Arabic name for Gabriel (ﷺ), the archangel who transmitted the verses of the Qur'an and other communication from Allah to Prophet Muhammad (ﷺ)
jihad (jihâd)	جهاد	struggle or striving (in Allah's cause)
jinn (plural of jinni)	جن	non-human, rational beings created by Allah from fire, often referred to as 'demons' or 'devils'; They have free will like humans: some are Muslims, others disbelievers; some are obedient to Allah, others disobedient. Satan is a jinni. Some people try to 'foretell' the future by contacting a jinni. Some disobedient jinn mislead people into thinking that they

can tell them what will happen in the future, near or far, or that the jinn can provide people with riches or some sort of power.

jizyah	جزية	a tax levied on the people of the Scriptures when they are under the protection of a Muslim government; it is in lieu of the alms tax paid by Muslims
Kaaba (Ka'bah)	الكعبة	the House of Allah in Makkah, originally built by Prophets Ibrâheem and Ismâ'eel, and which Muslims face wherever they pray
lâ ilâha illâ Allâh	لا إلَه إلى اللَّه	there is none worthy of worship other than Allah
madh-hab	مذهب	school of juristic thought
maḥram	محرم	a degree of consanguinity precluding marriage; a man whom a woman may never marry due to the close blood or marriage relationship. e.g., father, brother, son, uncle, and father-in-law
Ramadan (Ramaḍân)	رمضان	the ninth month in the Islamic calendar; the month of obligatory fasting; the month in which the first verses of the Qur'an were revealed
salâm	السلام	peace; the greeting of peace
sharia (shari'ah)	شرعة	Islamic law derived from the Qur'an and the Sunnah
shaykh	شيخ	teacher, mentor; scholar
shirk	الشرك	associating partners with Allah
soorah or soorat	سورة	chapter of the Qur'an

subḥân Allâh	سبحان الله	glory be to Allah
Sunnah	سُنَّة	the practice and collected sayings of Prophet Muhammad (ﷺ) that together with the Qur'an forms the basis of Islamic law
tâbi'oon (sg. *tâbi'ee*)	التابعون	those who knew or met any of the Companions and transmitted hadiths from them
tawḥeed	التوحيد	the Oneness of Allah: that He alone deserves to be worshipped and that He has no partners
Ummah	أُمَّة	community or nation: *usu.* used to refer to the entire global community of Muslims
unseen		a term used to denote phenomena or aspects that cannot be known using ordinary human faculties
uṣool al-fiqh	أصول الفقه	principles of Islamic jurisprudence
wali	ولي	friend and helper (of Allah); can also refer to a woman's guardian, usually her closest male relative on her father's side, who plays an important role in looking out for her interests and finding a suitable husband for her
zakât (*zakâh or zakât*)	زكاة	obligatory charity: an 'alms tax' on wealth payable by Muslims and to be distributed to other Muslims who qualify as recipients
zinâ	زنى	adultery or fornication

Notes

....

....

....

....

....

....

....

....

....

....

....